QUILT SAVVY

Gaudynski's
Machine Quilting
Guidebook

Diane Gaudynski

American Quilter's Society
P. O. Box 3290 • Paducah, KY 42002-3290
www.AmericanQuilter.com

Located in Paducah, Kentucky, the American Quilter's Society (AQS) is dedicated to promoting the accomplishments of today's quilters. Through its publications and events, AQS strives to honor today's quiltmakers and their work and to inspire future creativity and innovation in quiltmaking.

EDITOR: BARBARA SMITH
GRAPHIC DESIGN: ELAINE WILSON
COVER DESIGN: MICHAEL BUCKINGHAM
HOW-TO & SCENIC PHOTOGRAPHY: DIANE GAUDYNSKI
QUILT PHOTOGRAPHY: CHARLES R. LYNCH (unless otherwise noted)

Library of Congress Cataloging-in-Publication Data

Gaudynski, Diane
   Gaudynski's machine quilting guidebook : quilt savvy / by Diane Gaudynski.
      p. cm.
   Summary: "Detailed instructions for machine quilting. Includes techniques for freehand and free-motion designs. Detailed description of echo quilting and echo quilted feathers" -- Provided by publisher.
   ISBN 1-57432-900-6
   1. Machine quilting. 2. Machine quilting--Patterns. I. Title: Machine quilting guidebook. II. Title.
      TT835.G375 2006
      746.46'041--dc22

                                        2005034781

Additional copies of this book may be ordered from the American Quilter's Society, PO Box 3290, Paducah, KY 42002-3290, toll free 800-626-5420, or online at www.americanquilter.com.

Proudly printed and bound in the United States of America

Dedication

For my students, who take what I teach, make it their own, and soar with inspiration, creating quilts with a part of me in each one. Thank you all for giving back the gift a thousandfold.

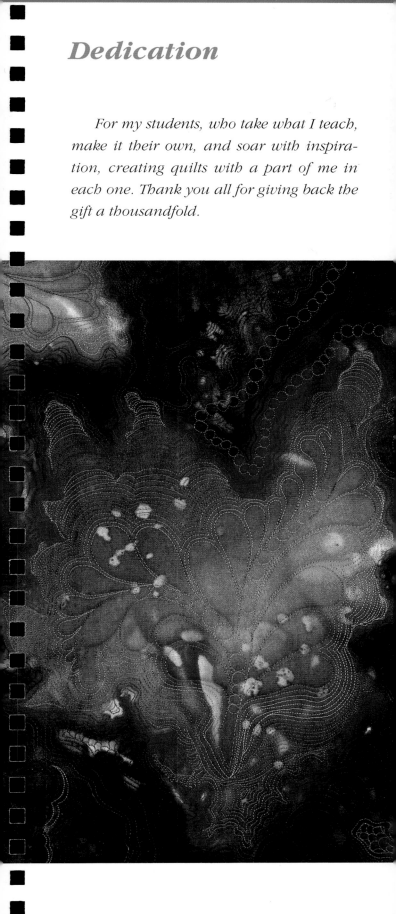

Contents

URN IN ABUNDANCE, 25" X 27", BY THE AUTHOR. COMBINING A MARKED TRADITIONAL DESIGN (PITCHER) WITH FREEHAND, INFORMAL QUILTING (BANDS INSIDE THE PITCHER) CREATES A RICH TEXTURE AND LETS YOU IMPROVISE AS YOU WORK.

Introduction

Making a quilt is a journey. Machine quilting it is high adventure! Before the New World was discovered, maps described the unknown geography as "a place where dragons be." That is exactly the feeling one might have when beginning to machine quilt: danger lurking, the unknown…but at the end, new worlds discovered.

We are at an amazing place in the history of quilting. We now have the tools, the skills, and the acceptance in the world of quilting to make a great top that is pieced, appliquéd, painted, wholecloth, pictorial, or whatever our hearts, minds, and hands can imagine and create, and we can machine quilt it and make it even better. It is a heady thought for many of us who began to machine quilt when it was not accepted in traditional work. Most of us saved machine quilting for quilt

tops we were not afraid to ruin. Machine quilting on traditional quilts was the black sheep of the quilting family, and now it has become something to admire, to respect for the skill required and its beauty, and to embrace with the knowledge that it is not second best but incredible in its own right.

From the pages in this book, I hope you will learn some new techniques and information to help you solve some of the most common problems encountered when learning machine quilting. Try one new background design, such as Bananas, and use it in a quilt. The sheer amount of it will reinforce your learning each time you sit and quilt, even if it's for just ten minutes a day. But you do have to quilt, and do try to quilt frequently so your skills are reinforced.

After completing a quilt with a new technique, that technique will be yours. It will be in your mind, in your muscle memory, and it will be a valued treasure to turn to again and again. It will also have your particular signature to it. It may not look like mine or like the photos in this book, but that's even better. Don't worry if your stippling looks like wood grain or your bananas look like papayas. I don't even know what a papaya looks like, but whatever your texture or fill becomes, it will be yours.

Look at the world around you with a quilter's eyes. You will see designs in everything—take notes and make sketches. Keep a journal or small notebook of ideas, or you will forget you had them in the rush of everyday life. Integrate quilting into your life and make it something that has priority. Quilting takes time, but the results are worth it. When you reach out and touch the texture you have created with machine and thread and your own imagination and when others value it, it is the best feeling in the world.

Quilting Styles

When I first began machine quilting in 1988, I noted that there was a dividing line between machine styles, one for traditional quilts and another for innovative, freehand, artistic quilts. There was some overlap in styles, but not much. Stippling was the main exception to this rule. It was used in both. Some basic techniques, such as loops, squiggles, and other free-form fills, may have wandered over the line and shown up in traditional quilts when the fabric was simply too busy for a traditional design. A traditional quilt required traditional quilting designs, and those tended to be hand-quilting designs, requiring a stencil or light box for marking, or new continuous-line versions of old favorites (In Fields of Gold, page 10).

Straight-line fills, crosshatch grids, and feathers with laborious and difficult backtracking were all part of the traditional style that a machine quilter would use. To add doodles to a reproduction 1800s' quilt was simply out of the question. In fact, I machine quilted traditional-style quilts for almost six years before I even allowed stippling to become part of the designs. Until that time, my backgrounds were lines, grids, and echo quilting (In Fields of Gold, page 10).

Marking the traditional quilt also was an issue and a difficult, time-consuming project. Finding markers that would last, that would show on busy cotton fabrics, and that would come out of the finished quilt was the endless quest. Products arrived on the scene that were better and worked well, but this style of quilting, with its intensive marking, still required an enormous amount of time spent tracing the designs on the quilt top. Machine

IN FIELDS OF GOLD, 83" X 83", BY THE AUTHOR.
THE ORIGINAL FORMAL-STYLE QUILTING DESIGNS
ARE BASED ON ANTIQUE PROVENCAL, WELSH,
ENGLISH, AND AMERICAN QUILTS.
PHOTO: Mellisa Karlin Mahoney, courtesy of *Quilter's Newsletter*
Magazine

trapunto added more time and required marking the designs before layering the quilt.

After working with students for many years, I realized I wanted to do some of the fun freehand quilting that I was teaching but that I forbade in my own work because "it just wasn't traditional." I decided the whole style issue needed some rethinking. Instead of "art" and "traditional" I started to think of quilting styles as "formal" and "informal," and there is a crossover or blurring of the lines between these two styles.

Formal quilting, such as that used on a traditional quilt, could indeed include some fun freehand designs within its strict boundaries. Informal quilting, such as watercolor, bargello, pictorial quilts, and art quilts, could also benefit from some more structured quilting styles, which might include feathers, straight lines, and interesting versions of crosshatch grids. No longer was there a right or wrong way to approach any particular quilt.

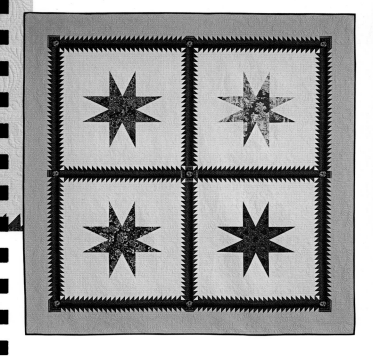

In addition, my students were more successful with these kinds of designs. The moaning and groaning were greatly diminished in classrooms everywhere. Feathers were finally attainable. Backgrounds became much more interesting. Markers were put back in the drawer. With the freedom to create designs that looked absolutely fine in a traditional quilt, came relaxation, better control, and more-even stitches. Machine quilting was fun and relaxing, and smiles were my reward.

FREEHAND FEATHERS ARE EASIER AND MORE FUN
THAN TRADITIONAL MARKED FEATHERS.

MY HELPER, HILLARY

Preparing to Quilt

L earning to quilt will be so much easier if you prepare for it. Be sure that your machine is in tip-top shape, cleaned and oiled, and that you have a straight-stitch (single-hole) throat plate. If you are using a puffier batt than normal, it is helpful to lessen the pressure on the presser foot. Sometimes there is a dial for this on the side or top of your machine. Check your manual.

Check to see if your machine needs oiling; most do. I clean out lint and debris from the bobbin area every three hours of steady use. At the same time, I also put a drop of oil on the hook race and run the machine for a few minutes to distribute the oil. Wipe up excess oil with a cotton swab. Regular oiling makes a big difference in the machine's performance, sound, and longevity.

Thread

To begin, use a practice sandwich with a non-busy fabric, so you can see what you've quilted. I use a very fine thread, #100 silk, but you can use a slightly heavier cotton, such as #60 two-ply embroidery, #50 Egyptian cotton, or any of the very fine cottons now available. I use one of these in the bobbin with the silk in the top, or the same thread in the bobbin and the top. Fine threads work best in these designs, because they don't cause knots and lumps easily, and they blend with the fabric beautifully.

Pick a neutral color for the bobbin that blends with or is the same as the top thread. Choose something for the top that is slightly different from the fabric, not matching, so you can see the designs as they form. With thin thread, it is exciting to use a color that isn't an exact match, and many times, it is much prettier because it creates a colorwash over the fabric where the quilting is dense. Sometimes secondary designs can form because of the thread build-up and the color.

SECONDARY THREAD DESIGN

Some thread ideas include using a pale-blue thread on a lilac fabric, or soft yellow or gold on lilac, pink, or ecru. Caution—one thing to avoid using is a very dark, fine thread on a light-colored fabric. It never ever looks good. The stitches can be spidery, fuzzy, and uneven looking and will showcase every irregularity in the machine stitch. Wobbles and slanted stitches will jump out at you. Backtracking will look like string. The deep color will obscure the stitches, so in fact, you cannot see your work better at all. Of course, dark fine threads look great on dark fabrics. Burgundy thread on burgundy fabric looks wonderful. Even for practice, avoid the dark fine threads on light fabrics. Trust me.

Needle

Choose the thread you like first and then the needle. For most of the threads listed previously, a #70 Microtex sharp needle works beautifully, leaving a precise small hole and creating a clean even line of quilting. I use a #60 Microtex sharp with the #100 silk thread, and it works very well, leaving tiny holes, but holes nonetheless. If the needle is difficult to thread or if the thread frays and breaks, the needle is too small for the thread choice. Go up a size. The indentation on the back of the needle is there for the thread to nestle in and form a perfect stitch, and if the thread is too fat for this groove, bad things, like skipped stitches and fraying, can happen.

Fabric Preparation

Prepare the fabric for these freehand design sessions by washing it. If it comes right out of the dryer fairly smooth, there is no need to press it. In fact, I prefer the feel of it unpressed. The backing also needs to be washed, and it should be a quality muslin or a good-quality cotton quilt fabric. Caution— avoid white-on-white fabrics for the backing because they do not move freely over the bed of the machine and will cause jerky, uneven stitches. If they are used as the top layer, the needle holes will be visible. Using a light spray of starch and pressing the backing really helps it glide over the machine when you move it.

Some quilt fabrics have dyes in them that make the fabric feel sticky, even when it is washed, so avoid these for backings especially. The beautiful commercial batiks are lovely but difficult to use for these lessons. They have such a heavy, tight weave that it is difficult to adjust the tension and to feel comfortable quilting. You need a bit of experience for these fabrics.

Batting

For the last few years in my quest to lighten up the weight of a quilt and to get loft without trapunto, I have used a wool batt (Hobbs Heirloom® wool batt). I really recommend it for these practice samples. The designs show up so much better than with cotton batts, and wool is so easy to quilt through. You will have better control because the quilt is so light and easy to move. When the quilt is finished, a light spritzing with water will make the designs grow a bit and be even puffier, and the backgrounds will be quilted down to almost nothing in thickness. The amazing thing is that the whole thing does not get stiff as a board but maintains its shape while having a nice drape. The softness of it will let you leave the "death grip" behind and gently hold and move the quilt under the needle. You may be able to give up gloves if you use this batt.

Sewing Machine Tension

If you are using finer-weight thread in the bobbin, the bobbin tension may need a slight tweak. A good rule of thumb: if you hold the thread with the bobbin hanging down, the bobbin should not drop. It might feel like it is going to at any moment, and that's generally where it works best. You can tighten or loosen the screw that controls the tension just a bit to get as perfect a stitch as possible. In every class I teach, I see at least one bobbin that is way too tight. If you do a sample of quilting with these finer threads and the stitches on the back look like they are strung tight—if it looks as if you could use that line of stitching as a guitar string—well, time to loosen the bobbin tension. Quilting put in too tightly will break, or cut and wear the quilt itself. All the bad rumors about threads probably come from incorrect tension and improper stitch length.

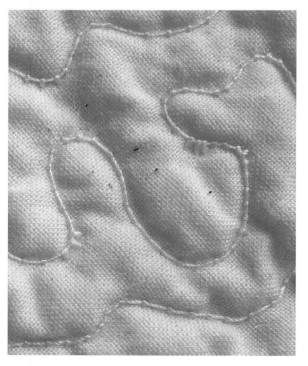

THIS BOBBIN THREAD IS TOO TIGHT.

TIP! If the color balance cannot be worked out, such as red on top, ecru in the bobbin, go ahead and put red in the bobbin as well. Some of the prettiest quilts I've seen had a variety of bobbin thread colors that created a whole new design on the back of the quilt. If you can balance the tension and not see bits of the other side's color showing, then it is fine to use only one bobbin thread color throughout the quilt.

Free-Motion Foot

For free-motion designs, visibility is crucial. A foot for your machine that has an open toe will give you that much needed view of the needle and where it is at all times. It also helps to have the shank of the foot offset to the right so the view behind the foot is unobstructed.

If you can't find an open-toed foot for your machine, you may be able to cut the front out of another foot (plastic or metal) to create an open toe. Also, replace large thumbscrews that obstruct your view with small

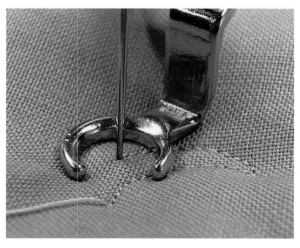

OPEN-TOED PRESSER FOOT WITH OFFSET SHANK

CUTTING THE FRONT OUT OF A FOOT WILL
INCREASE VISIBILITY

screws that are flush with the presser bar. Talk to your dealer and ask for assistance. It is so well worth it. Anything you can do to give you greater visibility as you quilt will make it easier and more relaxing.

Samples

Cut some 18" squares of the top fabric and the batting and cut the backing squares a bit larger all around. Pin-baste the layers with enough pins to keep it all together and to keep the corners from folding back and getting caught in the quilting. You can re-move some of the pins as you work and need open space. I don't use spray adhe-sives or fusibles because they make the quilt too stiff to handle easily. I can always tell on a sewing machine if they have been used, and many times, a little ball of sticky fuzz will build up on the needle.

It's overwhelming to some quilters to sit down to a square of blank fabric and begin quilting. It's best to divide the area into smaller sections. Sometimes drawing narrow border strips is good for practice, so that you can fit the designs into a space that is similar to what would be on an actual quilt. Give yourself plenty of room in each section, at least 4" to 6" square or sort of square if you are using flowing lines to subdivide the area.

TIP! Use the prettiest fabric. Don't save it for some future project. Learn to quilt on the very best. You don't need much, and you will be creating some fabulous quilted fabric that you can use for small projects. Handbags, pillow fronts, base fabric for appliqué, and small gift items can be made with this quilted fabric. Add some beading or crystals and you have a boutique item.

Generally, unless specified differently, it is easiest to build a design starting at the bottom of an area and work up or away from yourself. It is comparable to building a brick wall or stacking logs. It is also the way a plant grows. It sounds difficult but it is natural, and it's easier than fighting visibility by working toward yourself.

Let's get started. Prepare some gorgeous practice squares, oil and clean the machine, and get some great thread and new needles. Relax and breathe. The amazing thing about these freehand designs is they look nice even when you first try them. Using the right tools helps so much, and simply believing that you can create some interesting unmarked designs with a little guidance is the answer. It is definitely something even artistically challenged quilters can do. These are simple repeated shapes, creating puff and texture. Let yourself go, loosen up, and enjoy the learning. As soon as you feel you are doing fairly well, use the technique in a real quilt project.

Headbands

Many years ago, I saw a longarm version of this design I call "headbands." It was done over pieced traditional work, and I was amazed that something so simple could provide such a wonderful textured result. It worked much like any of the old-fashioned all-over designs, such as the fan, grid, circles, or even modern-day meandering. It covered everything, went over seams, provided a nice texture, and was not difficult

to do. The great thing about doing designs like this on the home sewing machine is that we have such control of our work that we can scale down large designs, touch lines of quilting already done, and make a simple design look intricate and lacy.

It is a case of visualizing the puff between the stitching lines and learning to control the speed so that thread knots don't form. We see the unquilted areas in the design, and to achieve a pleasing texture, it is crucial to watch the puff. Make it show! Keep it a bit uneven so there are different amounts of puff in the repeats of this design.

I named my version of this design "head-bands" because the base shape reminds me of those plastic headbands with the grippers underneath that gave me a headache in fourth grade. They still sell them, so if you need a visual, and your hair out of your face while you learn to quilt them, you might pick one up.

After the first headband, additional echoes of it are formed until you get as many of them as you want, then build another set. You can travel in any direction and add one or more headband shapes to take you where you want to go. They can even be quilted upside down. Even a beginner can learn this, but it is also a nice addition to the experienced quilter's repertoire.

Begin on a practice piece until you get the hang of it. Start by quilting a headband shape, about ½" or so, with the tips facing you. I refer to the tips as "garage A" and "garage B," and they are the points in the design where you take your foot off the gas and slow down. You don't have to come to a complete stop, because you are using fine thread, but you do need to slow down on the final approach to each garage. The open

BEGINNING A HEADBAND SHAPE

toe of the free-motion foot is a real asset
here. It helps you relax because you can easily see the touchdown point where you
bounce back into the next arc.

The only real problem I continually see
in classes is stitches that get too large on the
arc part of the headband. When you quilt the
arc, pull out in the passing lane and step on
it, remembering to keep up with your hands.
That's much easier than slowing down your
hands as you quilt this step. It's fun to go fast
on the big curves! Our machines are our
sports cars, and you need to drive them like
they were meant to be used. Remember,
hand speed and foot control pressure work
together to get even stitches. Don't even
think about cruise control.

As the arcs are completed and each time
you approach garage A or B, slow down
both your hands and the machine speed,
and touch a previous line of quilting. Be
careful not to crash through the far end of
the garage. You don't necessarily need to go
back to each starting point every time, but at
least touch a line of quilting to enclose the
design areas.

ENCLOSE EACH PUFF.

> **TIP!** Don't try for even headbands as you make them. It's prettier to have some fatter than others. We tend to make things way too regular. Try for some variety in the number of arcs, in the direction they face, and in the size of the puff you create in each. However, you do need to have even stitches. Those we want to be nice and regular.

Where do you make the second headband set? If you repeat the headband three times, begin the next set at either garage A or B, depending on the direction you want to go with the design. Sometimes it's fine to leave only one arc, or you can repeat up to perhaps five.

Another way to travel from one area to another is to echo around the outside of the designs until you get to the desired spot. You may also use a single headband or quilt short arc shapes to fill in spaces and gaps. Improvise; nothing is wrong as long as you keep consistent spacing and make it all blend. Occasionally, you may dead end, and then, alas, it's time to lock in the stitches

START THE NEXT SET AT GARAGE A OR B.

with six or seven very closely spaced stitches, and clip the threads. Move to a new area and begin again.

Headbands are great as a design. They can be small, large, or combined. They can be used instead of stippling or to give texture to the piecing and appliqué segments. Learning headbands lets you get the feel of your sewing machine and puts you in the driver's seat. No more one speed for everything. Headbands let you quilt with many speeds and get consistent stitches once you learn the connection between hand movement and foot speed. On the road of life there are passengers and there are drivers!

TIP! Make a small grouping of headbands, add a stem and some leaves and you have a great floral motif. They are also good for texture fill in the center of a floral appliqué, in sections of pieced blocks, or in narrow borders. You can also combine them with other puffy designs, such as feathers, for some variety.

Echo Quilting

When asked for suggestions and ideas on how to quilt something, I invariably respond with "How do you want to quilt it?" to find out the quilter's style preferences and skill level. And, oh, as an afterthought, I many times add, "You can always echo quilt it, and it will be perfect." After many confused, questioning looks from people, I have come to realize that many people do not know how to echo quilt and where it

will work. Echo quilting is the basis of most of the freehand quilting done either on a home machine or even on a longarm. It looks so simple and straightforward, yet it is more difficult than many overall designs because unevenness is instantly noticeable.

For me, it was my first staple in my grab bag of background quilting techniques. I was attempting to create the look of old-fashioned, everyday quilts, only done on the sewing machine. What I thought of as modern meandering or stippling did not seem appropriate to me then. I wanted something that did not need to be marked but which

would create dense backgrounds to make the quilted designs really stand out. Hawaiian quilters use echo quilting so effectively for this purpose, and I thought it would be a snap to do on my home machine. Think again! It is not the easiest skill in the world to master, so if you have tried it and been unsuccessful, perhaps my ideas will give you a second chance, because it is definitely worth the effort.

EXAMPLE OF ECHO QUILTING

What Is Echo Quilting?

To echo quilt, you use quilting lines to repeat the shape of a quilted design or an appliqué piece. The quilting lines, spaced about ¼" apart or less, are repeated around the design or appliqué, like ripples in a pond. They may exactly duplicate the shape of the object they surround, and then relax a bit with each new quilted line.

The lines of echo quilting are not marked, so you have to judge the space between each line and try to be consistent. Because this kind of quilting does not go in one direction but in many, you will quickly realize your free-motion skills need to include stitching sideways, at angles, even away from yourself, while maintaining nice, consistent stitches. I often compare this to the skill of juggling. Keeping all those balls in the air at once without dropping one or losing concentration takes a lot of practice until you can do it with ease.

Visualizing the Puff

After years of advising students to use the edge of the presser foot as a guide for even spacing, I suddenly realized that what we see in quilting is not the lines themselves but the negative spaces between the lines, or the puff. Two parallel lines create a nice ribbon of puff between them, and this is what we need to look at while keeping the spacing consistent. We need to try to manipulate the puff instead of looking at the ever-changing edge of a foot or some other arbitrary point of reference.

Visualizing this space as a sidewalk and trying to keep the sidewalk exactly the same width gave me the key to successful echo quilting. For some quilters, thinking of it as a silk ribbon has helped them look at the

WATCH THE SPACE BETWEEN THE LINES.

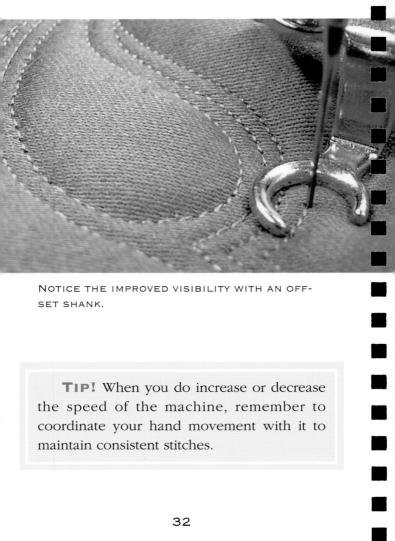

NOTICE THE IMPROVED VISIBILITY WITH AN OFF-SET SHANK.

TIP! When you do increase or decrease the speed of the machine, remember to coordinate your hand movement with it to maintain consistent stitches.

space. As another pleasant discovery, I can quilt much faster if I look at this space instead of the edge of the foot.

Echo quilting is so much like driving in changeable weather conditions. When visibility is impaired and you can't easily see where you are going, slow down. Then speed up on the long straight-of-ways where you can see a mile down the road. Learning to use a variety of speeds as conditions change will help you achieve expertise in echo quilting and in all free-motion techniques.

A really helpful tool for getting the space consistent, and that really is the secret to beautiful echo quilting, is a free-motion foot whose shank is offset to the right. With this type of foot, the view to the back is unobstructed. If your machine does not have a foot like this, perhaps it does have a free-motion foot that has plastic in this area so you can look through it to space the lines of echoing.

While the offset shank is the most important feature for a free-motion foot, it also helps to have one that is open in the front. It makes it easier to see the space in front of the needle and to judge the space from the needle to the previous line of quilting. I also prefer a small metal foot so that it doesn't cover much of the area and allows me to proceed with confidence because I can see what I am doing. Large plastic feet with closed fronts do not work well.

Where to Begin

Traditional hand echo-quilting lines are about ¼" apart, and each row stops and starts as a separate round. With machine quilting, it is so much more efficient to eliminate all these stops and starts.

To begin, insert the machine needle on the line of quilting to be echoed, or at the edge of the appliqué. Lock in the stitches with seven or eight very closely spaced stitches and angle out to the distance from the line you want to create as the space between lines.

Once you quilt out far enough, say ¼", then quilt at this distance all the way around the motif, without turning your quilting. After quilting around the motif once, continue by spiraling around it rather than making separate rounds. Keep the spacing consistent and move outward until the background area is filled. End the line of quilting by veering back to the previous line and overlap it a bit, locking in the final few stitches by making them very small.

Sometimes there will be areas that do not get filled in, such as corners, and you can go back to fill those in later. If an echo design ends in the center of an area, resolve it the best you can. Keep your spacing and end by overlapping another line of stitching, if possible. Lock the line of sewing with several tiny stitches as before. These little "puddles"

FILL THE BACKGROUND WITH ECHO QUILTING.

where echoes meet will form interesting designs in the background of your quilt.

Remember, if you have a large quilt rolled up in the machine, turning it is impossible. When you echo quilt, you need to learn to stitch in all directions without turning the quilt. Once you have mastered the skills of not turning the quilt, and stitching sideways and backward as well as toward yourself, you will be able to learn many other freehand fills.

Where to Echo Quilt

Usually, it's a good idea to select a technique for specific places in your quilt where it will solve problems as well as create a nice design. As a general rule of thumb, to help you decide, remember that echo quilting looks great where stippling might work as well. If it would be difficult to mark a background design such as a grid or lines, consider echo quilting.

If the areas to be filled with quilting are not connected or are very irregular, echoing would be difficult and stippling might be a better choice. One place echoing works very well is in the center of a feathered wreath. It will parallel the tops of the feathers and create a spider web effect. Give it a try!

> **TIP!** Border designs look tailored and lovely surrounded with echo quilting. However, echoing can stretch the outside edge of the quilt, causing wavy borders. It's a good idea to stay-stitch together the three quilt layers at the very edge of the quilt before echo quilting in a border.

When all the quilting is finished, some-times you will notice that the outer edges are no longer straight. Because cotton fabrics stretch and echo quilting is a bit like rolling out pastry dough, the edges will not stay straight even if they started out that way. To fix this problem, wet the entire quilt or just the borders, block the quilt, and let it dry. Then draw a new line for the outer edge of the quilt. The areas that have been pushed out by the echo quilting will be cut off when you trim the quilt after stitching the binding on the front of the quilt.

Sometimes echo quilting will push excess fabric along until you are faced with a bal-loon of fabric to be worked in. It is helpful to raise the presser foot a bit if possible, by decreasing the pressure on it. It will float over the bubble and not push it into pleats. Work at the ballooned area by encircling it, rather than quilting from one side to the other, "snowplowing" the excess along until it makes a pleat. If you think there is ab-solutely no way of avoiding a pleat, then switch to stippling in this area and work in the excess with this technique instead. Mix-ing these two techniques is a natural fit, because stippling is only echo quilting with a few bumps.

Echo quilting provides a wonderful tex-tured design that even beginners can do suc-cessfully. It really makes quilting motifs stand out beautifully, works well around trapunto and appliqué, and eliminates time-consuming marking for traditional backgrounds, such as crosshatch grids. It is perfect for traditional as well as folk-art appliqué.

Echo quilting will make a great way to begin a new year of machine quilting. Plan a project to include some echo quilting. Switch colors of thread to give it some zip. Play with it, and it will give you a lovely quilted effect as well as experience and skill that will transfer over to all your machine-quilting techniques.

ECHO QUILTING AND STIPPLING CAN BE USED TOGETHER IN A QUILT.

Echo Feathers

M ost machine quilters who have quilted traditional or formal-style heirloom
quilts have tried quilting feather designs, with
varying degrees of success. I learned early on
about speed, control, fine thread, feather
size, and frustration. Spines are the most difficult part to quilt, and they are the first thing

needed in a feather design to stabilize the area and to provide a base for the rows and legions of feather loops. Some days the quilting would go well—all the planets aligned, machine working, eyes in focus, hands under control. But other times, for some unknown reason, my attempts at backtracking over a previously stitched line to get to the next feather would fail miserably. I could only watch as my quilting disintegrated and my tension mounted.

Art quilters have it easy. They don't have backtracking in their informal feather style. They don't even quilt spines but form feather-like curves and shapes along a seam or an area of color. The loops flow and wander, thread mounts up here and there, and no one worries about it. We in the formal school of quilting are bound by a strict law to hit that loop with a second pass and make the backtracking undetectable.

I taught feathers for years, stressing the speed variation so that the students could slow down a bit and nail that backtracking then speed up on the next swoop of the loop. This proved difficult for 90 percent of my students. They also hated the fact that feathers had to be marked. They knew that over on the other side of machine quilting, the art side, the fun side, no one worried about marking the designs. Designs are free flowing and spontaneous, with various thread

TRADITIONAL FEATHER WITH PRECISION BACK-TRACKING

colors and weights. They flow like vines all over a quilt's surface. No one follows a marked line with backtracking. Rumblings of discontent were duly noted. Actually, I was becoming discontented as well because of the time-consuming marking process and because the marks don't last or are impossible to see.

One night around 2 a.m. I had a thought, and suddenly I was wide awake. I had a hunch that, if I took the best of both the traditional and art techniques, I would have a method that would not only be faster and easier but could be done on marked and unmarked designs alike. I would call them "echo feathers," based on the corridor I would leave between and around each loop, a small echoed "sidewalk" that would make them easier and faster, yet still traditional. Applying the concept to feather designs to put them within the reach of most machine quilters was the next step. I never got back to bed that night.

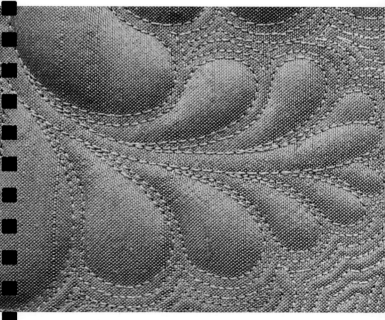

NOTICE THE CORRIDORS BETWEEN THE LOOPS.

Marked Feather Designs

Mark the design on your fabric with a blue washout marker. If you have used a stencil to trace the design, be sure to fill in all the gaps left by the stencil. You will need a solid line to follow while you are stitching the feathers.

Start by quilting the spine, following your marked design. Be sure to leave about a fat ⅛" corridor between the stitching lines. To add the loops to the spine, think of each one as a separate shape even though they touch. You will want to begin at the bottom of the feather design and work away from yourself. Start the first loop on the line, but as you quilt toward the spine to complete the loop, move inside the blue line.

Touch the spine and bounce back to the next loop to form a V at the spine. Retrace your path, but on the outside of the blue line, to start the next loop. The two lines of stitching will enclose the blue line between

MARKING THE DESIGN

43

LET THE BLUE LINE BETWEEN THE LOOPS
BECOME YOUR CORRIDOR.

ECHO QUILT DOWN THE OUTSIDE OF THE FEATHER.

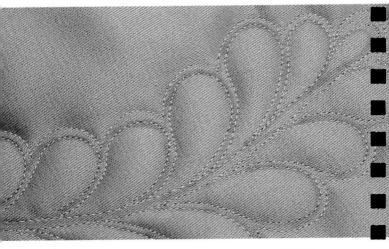

QUILT THE OTHER HALF OF THE DESIGN IN THE
SAME WAY.

the loops, and you will have a perfectly even corridor of about a fat ⅛". With some practice, this narrow space will look as if you had used a twin needle.

When one side of the design is finished, echo quilt back down along the outside curves of the loops. Leave a fat ⅛" space between the echo stitching and the loops as before.

Echo around the base of the spine, swerve in to touch the spine, then form the first loop going out to the other side. Again, complete all the loops, leaving a space between each one, and when they are completed, echo around the outside of the design on the second side. Echo quilting like this actually improves the original stencil design and makes the feathers more distinct.

> **TIP!** If you like, after the first echo, you can switch the thread color and continue adding echoes to fill in the background of the design.

Unmarked Feather Designs

The same basic method is used to quilt a feather design without marking. You do need to have the basic concept of the feather shape in your mind. It is sometimes helpful to do two things: mark the spine first so it is just where you want it to be and sketch in some lines for the outer boundaries of the loops.

The spine looks best and quilts more easily if it is placed on a bit of an angle, almost on the bias. Starting at the bottom and working away from yourself, quilt a line for the spine, curving it at the tip to create a shape that looks a bit like a cotton swab.

NOTE THE QUILL-PEN-SHAPED TIP.

Then echo back down the other side of the spine, ⅛" to a scant ¼" away. End the spine with a quill-pen-shaped tip, oval, or any other way you like. Slow down and meet the first stitches you made. You can take a breath here, re-grip the fabric (no death grip please, a light touch works best), and start the first feather.

> **TIP!** It's nice to add your own signature finials to your feather designs. Instead of the cotton swab at the top, try to quilt something more interesting. Start by really looking at lamp finials, drapery finials, the tops of wrought iron fences, etc., for design ideas.

Build the loops on one side as you would for a marked feather. If you use fine thread, all of the lines stitched to the spine will not build up or become unsightly. The thread will provide depth of color there, much like the center of a flower. With #100 silk thread, the effect is quite lovely.

Build loops of various sizes. They do not have to be uniform. In fact, the more irregular and organic they are, the more interesting and beautiful your design will be. If you keep the space between them consistent, the strangest looking loop will suddenly look great. You can travel along the spine for a bit and leave a gap or space where a loop may have fallen out. Keep it interesting and natural. Make the design your own.

TIP! It doesn't matter if you quilt the left or right side of a feather design first. Do whatever is most comfortable for you. Practice drawing the feathers first to train your brain and become comfortable with the path you will follow when you start working at the machine. Most of my students can do the left side better than the right, but with practice, you will be able to get both sides the same.

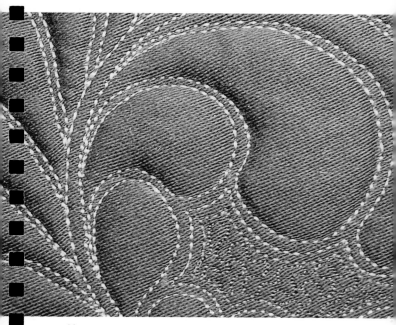

UNMARKED FEATHER QUILTED IN #100 SILK THREAD

Once you get to the top of the design, the cotton swab tip, you have two choices. Leave the swab as is, with no echo, or echo it once and then again to return to your pathway down the outer curved edge of the loops to the base. Merge the echo line back in with the previous stitching and lock in those stitches. You will have a beautiful, one-of-a-kind feather plume, tailored and elegant, fit for any formal-style of quilting or perfect for any style at all.

EXAMPLE OF A FORMAL FEATHER DESIGN

TIP! With a wool batt, which has a nice loft, I can now use the echo-feather technique instead of trapunto to make my feathers stand out. They aren't quite as plump, but the time saved by not marking some or all of my feathers and not having to trim away the extra trapunto batting more than makes up for any decrease in the feather "plumposity."

Bouncing Bananas

While machine quilting some doodling to work out any leftover oil from the hook area, I chanced upon a repetitive design for backgrounds or basic texture. It is based on two key elements: the arc shape of a banana and the bounce needed at each end of this shape to keep knots from forming on the front or back. If you learn the bounce and can form bananas, then you can create interesting background textures and designs. The design is based on the concept that the

repetition of a small arc creates a great texture, and it can be used to move you from design to design. An arc is far easier to quilt than a straight line, and the swirl where the bananas meet stands on its own as a design but also adds intricacy to the overall look. As long as the arc isn't too large, it is well within even a beginner's control level to create a smooth, even result. The banana design is a feasible alternative to stippling or more difficult traditional techniques, such as grids or straight parallel lines, and it requires no marking. It does sometimes help to practice drawing bananas first, so you know how the design builds when you start quilting.

> **TIP!** Use a fine thread in both the top and the bobbin so there are no messy thread pile-ups where the bananas converge. I like #100 silk or a very fine Egyptian cotton. Done on a larger scale, heavier threads can be used successfully.

The Basic Shape

This design is based on the simple shape of one banana. The subsequent shapes are added either to form a curvy bunch of bananas, with a definite stem end, or they are stacked, one on the other, to travel and to cover space. It is easy to quilt this shape because we all recognize it and have it in our mind's eye.

Start at one end, quilt a gentle curve about ½" long, and then change directions to complete the banana shape.

Continue from this starting point and immediately build another banana. The second banana does not need to extend as far as the first, and each subsequent banana can be nestled into the bunch and end in a different place.

The Bounce

The trick to having smooth joins where all the arcs converge is to approach the tip of each banana and immediately bounce in the other direction for the next shape. Do not linger at the tips. If you feel you are lost or don't know where to go next, don't keep running the machine while you decide. A knot of thread will build up quickly. Either bounce at the ends of the arcs and proceed into the next shape, or pause and run the machine for only a stitch or two and then move on, or stop the machine completely while you decide what the design needs next or where to proceed.

TIP! Be careful not to jerk your hands, but gently bounce into the next shape, much like a pool ball hits the side of the table and moves in another direction. Smooth slow hands are the key to beautiful quilting.

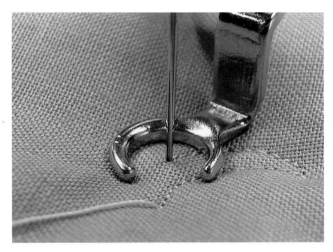

FORMING THE FIRST BANANA SHAPE

CREATING A BUNCH OF BANANAS

Building the Design

Two key things to remember are "pivot" and "stack." In the pivot, several bananas will begin or end in one spot. The resulting bananas form a swirl around a center point. In stacking, the bananas are built on top of each other. Their ends touch the previous banana but do not start or end in the same point. Both these techniques will build the design and keep it moving.

Unlike stippling, in which a pattern should not be obvious, in bananas there is a shape that is recognizable, and it can be repeated for short distances. Changing directions is vital to the overall look, and to do this, all you need to remember is pivot for a while then stack for a while. You can also quilt one banana in the opposite direction to change the look of the design, and then stack more arcs on that banana and pivot when needed.

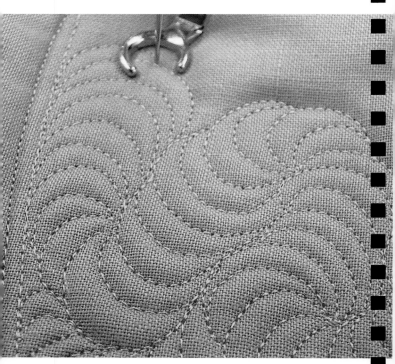

PIVOTED AND STACKED BANANAS LOOK A BIT LIKE A SLINKY TOY.

While many designs need fast and slow speeds for precise results, this design is so forgiving that many times I quilt it at a steady medium speed. You will gain speed as you become familiar with how the design works and builds. Try not to go all out or you will lose precision in meeting the previous line of stitching, and thread pile-ups can happen, or you can overshoot, making for a messy look. You want delicacy and precision so the design looks elegant and textured.

Where to Use Bananas

This technique is great for backgrounds you would otherwise stipple. It contrasts nicely with stippling used elsewhere in the quilt. It works well around areas that have many little parts and hard-to-reach spots. When surrounding a design, try to keep the bananas at an angle to the design so they stand out more.

THE RABBIT'S BACKGROUND CONTAINS BANANAS, DIANE-SHIKO, AND STIPPLING.

TIP! Using a thread that's a different color but the same value as the fabric makes this design really special. For example, use soft gold thread on rose fabric, blue on purple, or lilac on ecru.

Questions & Answers

Can this design be used for more than background?

If quilted with a contrasting thread color, the bananas can really stand alone as a design. By making the arcs larger and creating more puff, a wonderful overall design is created that can be easily seen. It may be used to fill areas of piecing and appliqué or as an overall design to quilt over the piecing to unify it. Try the design with a subtle variegated thread for an entirely new look.

Do all the shapes have to be the same size?

No, but they shouldn't vary wildly. Always keep in mind a bunch of bananas—some bananas are longer and thinner, some shorter and fatter, but all merge at the stem. You can always go back inside a banana shape and quilt another arc down the middle to divide the space into two smaller bananas, if your first one is incredibly puffy.

I have knots at the stem end of my bananas. What's wrong?

You either paused too long while running the machine fast at this point, or the thread was too thick for this style, or both. Try slowing down where points converge, or try learning this technique while using a finer thread. Once you get the hang of getting to an end point in the design and quickly bouncing off it to go into the next arc,

BANANAS CAN VARY IN SIZE SOME BUT NOT A LOT.

you will find that the knots start disappearing. Every time you think you are hesitating too long, stop the machine, take a breath, re-arrange things with your hands then start off again. You control the quilting; don't let it control you. It's a good idea to practice pivoting and stacking by drawing this design on paper to get the hang of it.

How do I travel to the various parts of the design?

Simply add bananas or arcs and bounce your way to a new spot. In other words, you want to banana your way over to a new area. Any small, repeated arc shapes will work as well.

Spirals and Clams and Fronds, Oh My!

Spirals

One of the age-old designs in all areas of the decorative arts is the spiral. It can be found in New Zealand and across the world, even carved in the stonework in Wales. I like to include this motif in my quilts for its beauty, its ease of quilting, and because of its symbolism.

It takes a bit of practice to learn it, but once you do, you will remember how to do it forever, and it will become a valued part of

your repertoire of quilting motifs. It doesn't require marking, but a marked boundary is helpful to keep the spirals even. They will look great in any part of your quilt or on a garment. Nothing limits them but your imagination.

Use spirals with other designs, whether marked or freehand, to add the appearance of complexity. Spirals can be subtle, or they can be very noticeable, especially when made with metallics or other specialty threads.

The basic spiral consists of quilting half a circle, smoothly spiraling in toward the center point, making a small curve around the center point, then spiraling back out of the circle. It sounds more complicated than it really

ADDING SPIRALS TO OTHER DESIGNS

COMPLETED SPIRAL UNIT

is. All it takes is a bit of practice drawing it and then some time quilting it on a practice quilt sandwich. I recommend drawing spirals with pencil and paper (pen is too slippery and you can lose control), but don't draw the spirals on fabric then try to quilt on the drawn line. If you imprint the path and the sequence in your brain, you will be able to quilt it more easily without marking.

I like to quilt my spirals from left to right, like I read. However, many people find it easier to quilt spirals vertically because it gives them greater visibility on their machines. That offset shank on my free-motion foot is fabulous for this design, because it provides optimum visibility and only one teeny blind spot at 2 o'clock. Sometimes, in a big quilt, because it is rolled up, you have no choice but to quilt the spirals in whatever direction they are going. Practice quilting in all directions, so you don't have to resort to turning a big quilt to do this simple design. This is a good mantra to repeat over and over: "Don't turn the quilt!"

Use a blue washout marker to draw two guidelines, about 1" apart, for your row of spirals. Start quilting at the midpoint within this path. You can add another blue line for the middle, if it helps.

STARTING A SPIRAL

63

START SPIRALING AT 3 O'CLOCK.

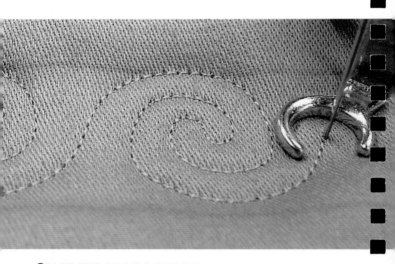

SPACE THE SPIRALS EVENLY.

ECHO ALONG THE TOP OF THE SPIRALS.

Quilt half a circle, beginning at 9 o'clock, up to 12, and around to 3 o'clock. Instead of completing the circle, start spiraling into the center.

When you reach the center, make a small curve around the center point. Estimate the space you left on the way in and divide it evenly as you quilt back out of the spiral.

Quilt down to the 6 o'clock position on the bottom guideline to end the first spiral. Notice the width of the corridor between the stitching lines inside the spiral. Use that same width between spiral units as well. A nice ¼" is easy to visualize and works well for learning. A greater distance between the lines will make it more difficult to maintain consistency. After that first spiral, do another one. The tops and bottoms of the spirals should hit the guidelines or at least the top line. Don't worry about touching the bottom one.

After you do a row of spirals, echo along the outside of them at least two times. It really enriches and completes the design, fills space, and camouflages any irregularities. Keep the spacing consistent, because the puff will draw the eye, and a fat puff will stand out too much and be distracting. Don't worry if the lines aren't perfectly spaced. They will all blend together because they are curves.

TIP! When quilting the first big curve, give it plenty of speed with your foot control, because your hands will tend to move too fast here. When you are doing the spiral part, you will be really concentrating and the hands will slow down. That's the time to back off on the foot pedal so the stitches don't pile up. It's hard to remember all this when you are learning the design, but in time, all the parts of it will fall into place nicely, if you really concentrate.

You don't have to do spirals in a row. You can include them in stippling to break it up and give it a fresh look. Try doing spirals here and there, arranged haphazardly, as a background. Don't worry too much about them. Done singly with no echo, they make great wave designs. Use your imagination. Any time I wonder what in the world to quilt in some obscure spot, I think "spirals!" They always look wonderful, and they are fun to do, but I do warm up a bit before I do them on my quilt. I tend to forget exactly how they go until I have done one or two.

> **TIP!** Instead of a circle, try spiraling with squares. It will form the Greek key design.

LEAF DESIGN WITH HEADBANDS AND FEATHERS

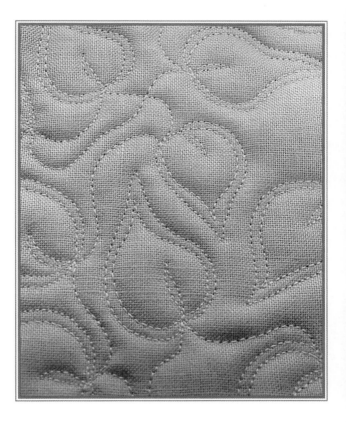

Leaves

There's nothing prettier than seeing natural shapes that we can recognize and that evoke thoughts of gardens, plants, and the outdoors. Adding these wonderful designs is easy even for beginners, yet they are sophisticated enough to include in our heirloom projects.

I like to include tiny leaves in unexpected places where some kind of design is needed. They also work well as an allover design to unify a quilt's segments. Leaves can also be used instead of stippling as background fill, to form wonderful free-form border designs, and to add here and there to feather designs to make them more graceful and interesting.

It's easiest to quilt a simple leaf shape, similar to the familiar philodendron leaf. Begin at the bottom of the design and work up or away from yourself. Moving in this

LEAF WITH SPIRAL STEM

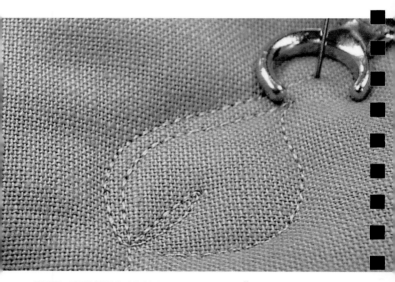

ECHO QUILTING AROUND LEAF WITH "CANDLE-FLAME" VEIN

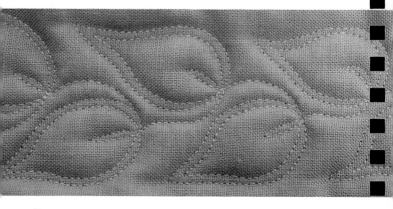

STRING OF LEAVES

direction is not only natural, it gives you better visibility while forming the designs.

The trick is to speed up with the foot control on the leaf shape so the stitches don't get overly large, then slow down at the base where the lines of quilting converge. I also stress that a simple echo around each leaf adds so much to the design for so little extra effort. Add a simple "candle flame" vein in the center and you are all set. Do a string of leaves, with a softly curving line between each one.

If you are adventurous, or really a botanical wizard, try other plant varieties. Go on a walkabout in your yard, park, or neighborhood and collect some specimens that you can use as models for your quilting. Using the types of leaves where you live makes the quilting so much more personal and imaginative. Gingko, maple, eucalyptus—use whatever you like that will work on your quilt.

Fronds

Another type of leaf design to try is a frond. Think of palms or ferns, some drying and browned or moving in the wind. I like to quilt a central vein first from bottom to top, echo it back down to the base, then work up to the tip again, adding the individual leaves on one side. When I reach the top, I echo the vein again down to the base on the other side so the vein has three lines, then complete the leaves on the opposite side, working again from the bottom up.

Make the leaves uneven and natural. Work out from the center vein and as you approach it after completing each leaf, slow down and just touch it before bouncing back into the next leaf. Quilt each one differently. Create some long wavy ones, some shorter spiky ones, and mix it up. If you have the

COMPLETED FROND DESIGN

center vein undulate through an area of your quilt, it will fill the area nicely, with no background quilting needed. This frond design looks nice on the edges of garments, especially when it is done in a specialty thread.

> **TIP!** An undulating frond works great on a batik, a print, and all green fabrics. It blends in beautifully and needs no marking. Sketch in the center vein if you want, but keep it a natural wave, not an exactly even repeat.

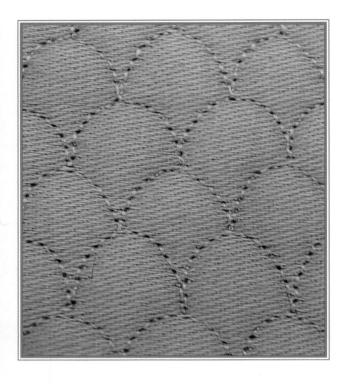

Clamshells

An age-old quilting design is the clam-shell. It is marked with either a single tem-plate repeated over an area or with a stencil that includes all the clamshells lined up. You can also make clamshells by using half of a found circlular object. If you see an extensive-ly quilted vintage quilt, chances are, some-where in the intricate quilting, you will find clamshells.

For large clamshells in machine quilting, it is still a good plan to mark them with a tem-plate. However, for a small clamshell fill, it's not at all difficult to quilt them freehand. Again, some guidelines might be helpful. Marking lines about ⅜" apart and using them as pathways to fill with clamshells helps keep them even and lined up nicely.

I rarely mark this small design, and I use it all the time. When something looks not quite complex enough, or maybe it needs a little extra something, I add clamshells as an edging. I discovered while quilting and

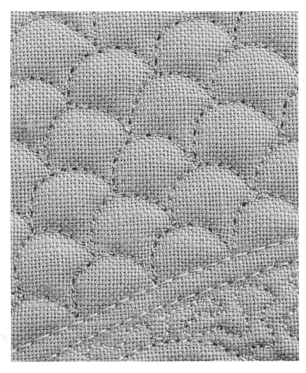

CLAMSHELLS USED AS A BACKGROUND FILL

CLAMSHELL EDGING AROUND A MOTIF

teaching that we are almost always repetitive and organized in our work. If we make one shape, the next one tends to be just the same. It's difficult for me to be random, to vary the sizes of my motifs. They can easily look as if they were spit out by a computer, all lined up and the same if I don't concentrate. This is one design for which that tendency comes in handy.

To build the design, begin at the bottom. Think of building a brick wall. You lay down the bottom row of bricks. Then each brick in subsequent rows will be offset, straddling two of the bricks below. There is a natural flow to the design as you work. Each clamshell, or half circle, allows you to pause briefly before doing the next. I think of each shape as a bunny hop. You move along the row, hopping, touching the previous row, bouncing off to the next half circle, breathing, and moving on again. You establish a rhythm. Don't look at the needle, but try to go up the same amount for each half circle.

When you reach the end of an area or row, travel in the ditch, on the stitching of a neighboring design, along the raw edge of the quilt, wherever, to go to the next row. Aim ahead at the center of the next shape.

TIP! Visualize the puff you are creating as the perfect half of an orange instead of looking at the line you are quilting.

Make as many rows as you want to fill an area. Estimate the space left and adjust the sizes of the last few rows so they will fit in nicely. This takes a bit of experience, but even if it doesn't work out exactly and you have one row with slightly differently sized clamshells, not to worry. It all blends in.

You can probably do up to ½" clamshells on a home machine, and larger, of course, on a longarm and still keep them consistent. Clamshells smaller than ½" will simulate snakeskin. Larger clamshells look like roof tiles. Fish scales can also be mimicked with clamshells. They make a great fill in sections of piecing and appliqué, and they work as background, too. I tend to prefer them quilted in something enclosed so they line up well.

SMALL SHELLS LOOK LIKE SNAKESKIN OR FISH SCALES.

Circles

A few years back, I wanted to try to get some feather designs to look like those in the antique quilts from Provençe. They had tiny circles or ovals, which looked like pearls, quilted in the spine of each feather, which added so much intricacy and beauty to the small pathway.

I decided to give it a try and knew immediately, as I was holding my ¼" circle template, that there was no way I would try to mark them all with the template. I came up with the idea that, as long as the shapes were all enclosed and there were boundaries to

follow, I could quilt them freehand, in any direction the spine went.

For practice, I stitched a corridor of two parallel lines about ⅜" apart. Beginning at the left in the center between the lines, I quilted a clamshell for half the first circle. I continued quilting clamshells all along inside this narrow pathway, ending each one at an imaginary midpoint in the spine. When I reached the end of the corridor, I continued the last clamshell and envisioned a full round circle in my mind and tried to quilt the bottom half with an upside down clamshell.

It worked wonderfully. By imagining that circle instead of watching the needle, I was creating the negative space, or the puff. It was so much easier than marking, and I found that, if I went at a slow controlled speed and moved my hands smoothly, the circles built rapidly and looked even and smooth. It took a few circles to get the hang of it, and I still warm up first when doing this design, because it requires quite a bit of concentration.

START CIRCLES AS CLAMSHELLS.

QUILTING THE BOTTOMS OF THE CIRCLES. THE ROUND SHAPE OF THE FOOT WILL HELP YOU IMAGINE THE CIRCLE SHAPE.

Remember that this is a design done free-hand by a human being, so the circles won't be perfect. They are like freshwater pearls, just a bit off but still gorgeous. You will improve as you quilt more of these. Soon you will be able to quilt them vertically, at an angle, or however the pathway takes you. I used this technique for the first time in my quilt IN FIELDS OF GOLD (page 10) and smiled the entire time I was quilting the circles, knowing it was special for this quilt. It made me very happy to quilt and see them.

> **TIP!** You can add these tiny circles to informal quilting styles as well. Simply quilt two parallel lines anywhere in your quilt and fill them with circles (see page 75).

It's best to wait until you are warmed up and fluid in your quilting before tackling circles. Then do all the circles in your project at one time. Don't stop and do another motif, then circles, and back to something else. You really become proficient if you repeat the same design over and over.

These designs are but a tiny sampling of all the freehand motifs that are out there for you to discover. Look around you, check out designs in your surroundings. Every hotel I go to I notice the carpet immediately, or the tiny swirls on the chair upholstery or the draperies. Motifs in jewelry or picture frames, dishes, fabrics, and laces may inspire you to come up with your own.

Quilting is never dull and boring, and it provides us the opportunity to make each quilt unique with our own "handwriting" of designs. Doing them freehand is the ultimate way of adding that extra personal touch.

RABBIT IN GREEN, 40" x 40", BY THE AUTHOR. THIS TWO-COLOR WHOLECLOTH QUILT IS MADE OF SILK DUPIONI, WITH A WOOL BATT AND SILK THREAD.

Diane-shiko

Straight lines and crosshatch grids are the mainstay of formal quilting. They are used for backgrounds, fills, and texture. However, for free-motion machine quilting, they are truly difficult. I usually explain to my students that, if you have two pictures on the wall and one isn't exactly straight, you will see it instantly and register that it is "wrong." The same is true of free-motion straight lines. It is difficult to keep them precisely straight and keep grid squares even. Marking all the lines is time consuming, and even then, it is difficult to quilt smoothly on the marked lines and in all directions without turning the quilt.

I was demonstrating the continuous-curve technique, which I had learned years ago from Harriet Hargrave, when inspiration struck. I had marked a small grid and was

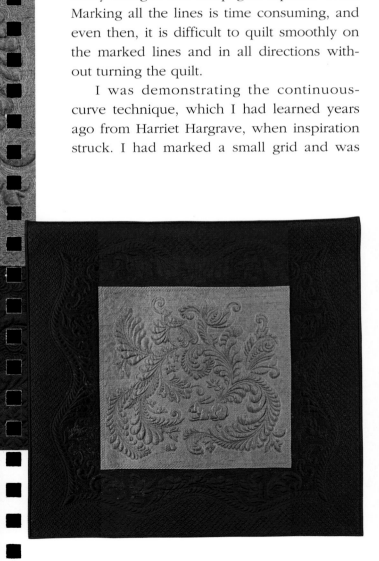

quilting continuous curves around the grid. I explained to my students that they should think of the marked lines as seam lines because the technique is really used for quilting pieced squares. Suddenly, I thought to myself, wow, you could forget the pieced squares and use the technique to quilt a background design. It looks a bit like cathedral windows, a double wedding ring design, a teacup or wineglass motif, or the lovely Japanese technique of Sashiko. A friend dubbed it "Diane-shiko."

It appears that you have quilted overlapping circles, but in practice, all you must learn to quilt is one simple arc, from one grid intersection to the next. Beginners can quilt the curves in Diane-shiko fearlessly and, with a bit of practice, get spectacular results. Since that day, I have used this continuous-curve grid design in several quilts and vests, and no matter how difficult the other techniques are in the piece, it is always this design that gets noticed and complimented. Yes, it takes a bit of marking, but the evenness of the results is so worth it.

Marking the Grid

I recommend that you practice this technique on a small quilt sandwich before using it on your quilt. The easiest way to learn this technique and to create the nicest looking results is to use a $1/2$" crosshatch grid. You can go up to a 1" grid, but this larger size is more difficult for a beginner. I have used a $3/8$" grid for smaller backgrounds or fills, and that's a great size to work with, too. Mark the grid on point, that is, at a 45-degree angle to a straight line in the quilt. It can also be quilted along the grain lines, but it is certainly easier to quilt if you do it on the bias, and it looks prettier, too.

There are several options for marking the grid. First, you can use a rotary ruler with a 45-degree line. Align the 45-degree line of the ruler with a straight line in the quilt, such as a seam line. Move the ruler along and mark at $\frac{1}{2}$" intervals, checking the alignment as you go.

The best option for marking is a grid stencil with slots cut in it every $\frac{1}{2}$". Instead of having to move a ruler for every line, with this tool, you can mark about ten lines at a time before repositioning the stencil. Besides being fast and easy, it keeps the lines perfectly aligned as well. Check your stash of notions because you may own one of these stencils and never found a use for it. If you have one, it is your lucky day because it makes this technique a snap.

You could also use a regular crosshatch grid stencil, which is okay, but the important part of the grid is the intersection of the

USING A GRID STENCIL WITH SLOTS

QUILT AN ARC BETWEEN THE GRID INTERSECTIONS.

SEW IN A SERPENTINE PATTERN FROM INTERSECTION TO INTERSECTION.

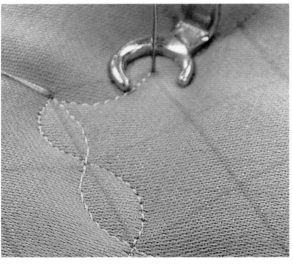

SERPENTINE BACK THE OTHER WAY TO FORM THE "FOOTBALL" SHAPES.

lines. Sometimes these stencils have gaps at the intersections, and it is time consuming to go back and draw them all in.

I use a blue washout marker to draw the grid on my quilts. On darker fabrics, a white iron-out pen is very good. It provides a clear, fine white line that is easy to see. It's important to use a good marker so the lines are visible and easy to remove. Big, fat, fuzzy chalk or blue lines don't work, nor do fine-line markers, which can drag on the fabric, almost scratching it. In addition, the resulting line can be indistinct.

Quilting the Grid

Because the arcs are not marked and are sewn freehand, they are easier to do for most quilters than following along a marked design. Once you establish how far out to swing the arc and you are happy with the size, you are all set and can sit and quilt arcs for hours.

The important parts of the grid to use as guides are the intersections where the horizontal and vertical lines cross. To quilt an arc, drop the feed dogs on your machine. Begin at one of the intersections, look to the next one and quilt a gentle arc, about a fat $1/8$" out from the marked grid line. Look ahead of the needle and aim for that next intersecting point.

When you reach the intersection, continue on and make another gentle arc, only on the other side of the line. Continue going from one side of the line to the other, forming a serpentine wave along one grid line.

When you reach the end of that line, you will have completed half of the arcs. In the same manner, complete the other half by working away from yourself and quilting up the grid line to form the "football" shapes.

To get to the next line, simply quilt an arc sideways over to the line. You can travel from line to line that way.

It is fine when you are learning this technique on a sample to quilt all the vertical lines first, turn your work, and then quilt all the horizontal lines. However, when you are working on a real quilt, it is best to quilt without turning your work, so you will want to practice quilting side to side.

NOTICE THE SIDEWAYS ARCS CONNECTING THE ROWS OF FOOTBALLS.

LEARN TO QUILT SIDEWAYS INSTEAD OF TURNING YOUR QUILT.

TIP! If the grid is marked on point, it will be easier to see and quilt the lines going both directions. Try it and see if the visibility improves.

When all the lines have been quilted, look at the design. Depending on how you look at it, the design is a four-petaled flower or overlapping circles.

COMPLETED DIANE-SHIKO SECTION

JOY, 22.5" X 28", BY THE AUTHOR. THIS ORIGINAL
DESIGN IS DONE IN HAND-DYED COTTON WITH A
WOOL BATT AND SILK THREAD.

Let's Get Real

In the real world, you will seldom get a nice setup like your practice piece. Instead, on your quilt, the grid may be enclosed within an already quilted area that is irregularly shaped. Here are some guidelines so you will know how to tackle it.

TIP! When marking an actual quilt, be sure to fill the entire space with marked lines, even if you have to overlap an already quilted area of the design. Better to have the marked guidelines overlap the design than to be quilting along and come to a gap with no line to follow.

It's a good idea to begin quilting the grid at the midpoint of a large area to stabilize it first. You can then use a ricochet technique to travel from one place to another; that is, instead of quilting back up a line to complete the football shapes, you can move to a nearby line. Or you can quilt on only one side of a grid line (making half footballs) as far as you want, then backtrack on the other side of the line to complete the football shapes. I like to work in an area that is small enough to be easily moved under the needle without repositioning my hands. I call this area my "working space." It's also easy to make half footballs along an entire border, which helps to stabilize it.

If the Diane-shiko grid lies next to an already quilted design, begin the grid quilting next to the design and work your way out toward the raw edge of the quilt. Doing so will work any excess fabric out toward the raw edge. If you try to quilt from an outside edge toward a quilted area, the presser foot will push the fabric along like a snowplow, and any excess fabric will bunch up at the design to form a pleat. As another solution, if you place the grid on point, you will be quilting with the bias grain, which will help keep a pleat from forming. I know it seems counter to all the logic, but in machine quilting, straight lines work best if placed on the bias.

TIP! If you are quilting the footballs with a different color of thread than the one used in the already quilted design, echo the design once with the football color. Then, if you have to move along the edge of the design to reach another grid line, you can travel along the echo quilting, so the traveling stitches won't be noticeable.

Fill in the quilting line by line. Sometimes, you will quilt all the lines in one direction then quilt the cross lines. Sometimes you will zigzag, following the lines where they take you. If you dead end, just cut the threads and move to a new place to begin again. When you are finished, turn the piece over so it is easy to see if you have left any unquilted lines or "orphans."

Questions & Answers

What happens at the edges when you cannot complete an arc?

Simply quilt as far as you can, stop and travel on a line of quilting, in a seam line, or along the outer raw edge of the quilt. For example, if the arc is interrupted by a quilted motif, such as a feather with echo quilting, stop and travel a short distance on the echo quilting to get to the next arc.

TRAVEL ALONG THE EDGES OF DESIGNS. NOTE THAT THE LAST LINE OF ECHO QUILTING IS THE SAME THREAD COLOR AS THAT USED FOR THE DIANE-SHIKO.

These cut-off football shapes will create the illusion that the quilted design has been placed over the background, and you can imagine the background continuing on underneath the design. It's a bit of smoke and mirrors that creates a layered illusion, always something good in quilting. It takes only a bit of practice to get used to ending the football shapes and fitting them in nicely.

My football shapes are way too fat— what happened?

You curved out too far when quilting each arc. Within a grid of $1/2$" spacing, a fat $1/8$" arc is plenty. If you are working on a 1" grid as the base, you can curve out a little more to make a fatter football. Sometimes you may feel more adventurous and tend to make fatter arcs. This does take a bit more concentration to be consistent.

I keep missing the intersections. What's going wrong?

You are probably going too fast. Try doing it again, but at a slower speed. Slow your hands down, too. This is a Sunday stroll in the park, not a racetrack.

There are knots on the back at each intersection. Help!

When switching over to the other side of the marked line at the intersection, you ran the machine at the same speed as when making the arc, but at the intersection, you hesitated to think about where to go next. Therein lies the problem. If you hesitate with your hands, but continue to run the machine at the same speed, you will build up a knot in just a few stitches. Fine thread helps but doesn't eliminate this pilot error. Concentrate on working the foot pedal and your hands so you slow down both and speed up both together.

What thread color works best, matching or contrasting?

When you match the thread to the background fabric color, the quilting creates a subtle background texture. If you choose a slightly different color from the fabric, the quilting will stand out more. A total stand-out, such as white or ecru on navy will definitely create a new look. The Diane-shiko will become the design, not the background.

Is this kind of quilting hypnotic?

Yes, it is. And because it is so repetitive, you will tend to lose your concentration and start making mistakes. Limit the time you do this and take breaks from it. It's easy, but it can look sloppy very quickly if you don't pay attention.

HELPER #2, ARNIE

93

ESPRESSO, 46" X 47", BY THE AUTHOR. MADE FOR THE PILGRIM AND ROY CHALLENGE AND AUCTIONED TO BENEFIT THE MUSEUM OF THE AMERICAN QUILTER'S SOCIETY IN 2005.

Dispelling Myths

D ispelling some myths, learning some simple aids and techniques, and tackling the job in an organized and informed way will allow you to master free-motion quilting. Sometimes, letting go of preconceived ideas of how all this should work can make the biggest difference of all.

Myth number one: *The quilt must be rolled tightly and secured with clips for free-motion quilting.*

Try not to be too tidy in packaging a quilt for free-motion work. Yes, long lines of walking-foot quilting should be sewn from top to bottom or corner to corner, with the quilt rolled into a tube so it can be guided successfully under the machine arm.

However, for free-motion quilting in specific areas of the quilt, this roll will only get

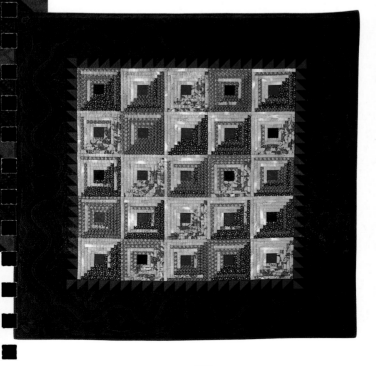

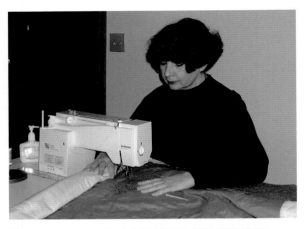

ROLLING A QUILT WORKS WELL FOR WALKING-FOOT QUILTING.

BUNCH THE QUILT UP AROUND THE AREA YOU PLAN TO QUILT.

QUILTING IN THE CENTER OF AN 85" SQUARE QUILT

in your way. You do have to continue to roll, fold, pleat, or scrunch up the portion to the right of the area you are quilting so that it fits in the opening of the machine, but the remainder of the quilt to the back and left should not be constrained in a tidy bundle. It will become a dead weight, a log, the tail of an alligator, as you try to move a small area under the needle to do a free-motion design. Instead, spread out the remainder of the quilt and distribute its bulk around the back and left side of the machine. Then bunch up an area around the needle—a bit like sandbagging a levee or making a "mashed-potato gravy lake." You will be quilting in the center of the area you have surrounded with hills of gently mushed-up quilt sandwich.

Much of the rest of the quilt can be mounded up in your lap. The area you are quilting should move freely while you rest your arms on the cabinet or, even better, on the padded surface the quilt itself provides. Don't hold your arms up in the air, but instead, let them rest, and use your fingertips and hands to control the work and move a small area of the quilt under the needle. Get comfy and snuggle into that soft quilt as you work.

Test it out to see if the area under your needle moves freely. If not, readjust the quilt so that there is no pull or drag and then proceed to quilt this area. If you feel even the tiniest tug or pull as you quilt, stop and readjust the mushed-up quilt so that its weight doesn't affect the area you are moving.

Myth number two: *You must press down firmly, hands flat on the quilt.*

Sometimes this is absolutely necessary, but most of the time, it's a hindrance to making smooth, even stitches. A firm but light touch works best to move the quilt easily. Continually pressing down hard with flat palms can cause jerky movements, resulting in uneven stitches, frustration, and cramped muscles. Try to rest your arms if possible and press down lightly with fingertips rather than palms.

It is a pressing and lifting combination that works best for your hands. You need a repertoire of hand positions to choose from for different tasks in machine quilting. There is no one perfect grip for everything. If the quilt is positioned correctly and the surface of the area under the quilt is smooth and

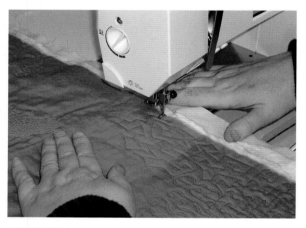

DEVELOP A REPERTOIRE OF HAND POSITIONS.

slippery, moving the quilt with your fingers offers the most control, creates the most even stitches, and decreases muscle strain.

Myth number three: *You need to wax the surface of the machine bed and surrounds.*

Over the years that I have taught machine quilting, I have heard many solutions to the sticky-surface syndrome. Guitar wax, home-appliance wax, spray this, and spray that. I have never had a problem with a sticky surface either on my machine or the surround that fits around the free arm, probably because I never use products like these or clean with chemicals. All these things can cause lasting damage and create permanently tacky surfaces.

If I do have to clean the Plexiglas® or machine bed, I use plain hot water on a terry cloth, or a bit of white vinegar to dissolve any starch residue. If the Plexiglas surround arrives with a label or covering that leaves adhesive residue, plain hot soapy water gets it off. Polish it dry with a clean flour sack towel. Even paper towels sometimes leave a residue, as does fabric softener.

Some of the new machines like mine have a bed of stainless steel that is the most slippery surface I have used. A surface like this can really improve your skill level fast. Also, there is a product on the market, a very slippery sheet called the Free Motion Slider®. It is the size of a piece of copy paper, and it's taped over the throat plate. I was delighted by how easily the quilt moves with this sheet.

The sheet also works well for trapunto if the poly batt won't move smoothly or if the backing fabric has dyes or a texture that doesn't slide easily. Beware of the popular white-on-white background prints because the print designs act as little grippers, and the quilt will not slide easily. I refer to this as "rubber fabric," and it does feel like it has rubber grippers on it. If you already have a project with this fabric as the backing, try using the reverse side of the fabric and one of the Slider sheets.

Myth number four: *Machine quilters go at breakneck speed and finish projects within hours.*

Watching longarm quilters work at speed probably adds to the idea that we at home machines do it the same way. Sometimes we do, but we are human beings and not computer-controlled machines. We need to work at a speed that is relaxing and comfortable, a speed that enables us to do controlled, beautiful work.

There are techniques to streamline the process by using efficiency rather than speed. The ultimate question I have students ask themselves when doing machine quilting is "Could I be doing this faster by hand?" If the answer is yes, then they are bogged down in inefficient techniques, even though they may be speeding away on the machine. There are so many little things you can do if you stop and think about efficiency.

One of the most inefficient uses of our time while working at the machine is stopping and starting, which involves pulling up the bobbin thread, making sure it passes through the foot correctly, checking the thread pathway so it is coming off the spool smoothly without catching anywhere, double checking that the thread passes through all the correct nooks and crannies on the machine, locking in the stitches, clipping or burying the threads so they don't show, picking up your rhythm again, and finally, making the whole process undetectable, front and back. Not only is all of this time consuming, but also it is inherently frustrating. It can definitely cause stiff muscles, loss of temper and patience, and a less-than-perfect-looking quilt.

I try to end a line of stitching and cut the threads as seldom as possible. I do stop and start often to readjust my hands, re-bundle the quilt, and take a breather. The needle is in the down position when I stop, so that the quilt will not move.

When I resume quilting, I begin by moving the needle to the up position and slowly stepping on the accelerator to move to normal cruising speed once again. Resuming quilting with the needle in the down position can often result in that little back and forth stitch. The needle seems to leap out of the quilt with a will of its own, and you overcorrect until several bad stitches have been made. Stopping to remove these stitches is time consuming.

Machine quilting should be relaxing and fun, not stressful. Check your fabrics, surround, packaging, and presser foot to make sure everything is set up for you to succeed and enjoy this fantastic technique.

HELPER #3, FLUFFY

Back Problems

So often, machine quilters complain of back problems from the hours spent at the sewing machine, but I'm referring to the problems on the backs of quilts, not quilters. Knots are a common problem, an unintentional embellishment I like to refer to as "acorns" or "thinking caps." If you look at the back of your quilt and discover these little lumps of thread, a word of caution—don't use sharp scissors to surgically remove them. Chances are, the line of quilting will eventually come out, and you will be left with missing stitches everywhere. There are several things that cause these acorns to form.

Thread Weight

Heavy thread in the bobbin only allows about two stitches in one spot before a knot develops. The minute you slow your hands to think about where you will be quilting next, or hesitate when trying to follow the design, a little thinking cap of thread will form.

Any thread from a three-ply #50 cotton and heavier is too thick for the bobbin when the quilting lines are close together. A #40 cotton, many times labeled "machine quilting thread," is even heavier and may create knots even faster as well as contribute to problems with machine tension.

The best bobbin threads are lightweight yet strong, and they are either cotton or polyester. Generally, for all machine quilting, I prefer an Egyptian #50 cotton that "reads" much like a #70 cotton thread, very fine. A two-ply #60 cotton embroidery thread with a silk finish is also a good choice. Some manufacturers are creating new bobbin threads especially for machine quilting. Look for threads specifically labeled for bobbins.

You may need to tweak your sewing machine's tension settings when switching to some of the finer-weight bobbin threads. If your machine doesn't like one of them, try another thread and see if that works better.

For a bit of magic, use a good quality invisible thread in the bobbin. I keep invisible thread on hand as one of my favorite tricks to use for a variety of tasks, such as stitching in the ditch or quilting over a multi-colored fabric.

THIS THREE-PLY #50 COTTON BOBBIN THREAD WAS TOO HEAVY FOR THE AMOUNT OF DETAIL. THIS THREAD EVENTUALLY BROKE.

> **TIP!** Although the front of a quilt may look perfect, the back can look horrendous. You might not know problems are happening until the thread or the needle breaks. Check the back often and change what you are doing if knots are forming.

Speed

Thread weight and speed work hand in hand. If you are using heavier threads, it is imperative to keep moving and not slow down or stop in one spot. The moment you do, that pesky thinking cap will form on the back. If you are doing widely spaced designs and can keep moving while quilting, heavier thread will work just fine because the steady speed will prevent knots.

For most quilters, however, to keep moving is not realistic. In the real world of machine quilting, you definitely have to slow down to see the marked design, and when doing freehand quilting, there is no marked design. Somtimes, slowing down or going out of control are your only choices.

To help prevent these speed problems, plan your route ahead of time. Familiarize yourself with the pattern. Trace the route with your finger. Teach your brain where you are planning to drive the machine, and if you get lost, stop! Instead of running the machine in one spot like idling the car engine while waiting for your navigator to read the map, stop and decide where you are going then resume quilting.

Repetition

To improve the quilting on the back, as well as the front, you need to repeat a design or motif until you become smooth and proficient. Warm up first on a practice sample you keep near the machine then proceed to quilting on a real quilt. Quilt all the motifs that are the same, one after the other, no matter where they are in the quilt. This repetition will give you muscle memory and teach hand speed and simultaneous control of the foot pedal. You will learn the route of the design, where to pause, and which way to go, so there will be fewer knots every time you quilt a particular design.

Machine quilting takes more than just knowing how it is done. It takes hours of repetition so that it becomes an automatic skill the body learns, much like walking, riding a bike, typing, or playing a musical instrument. Next time you sit down to machine quilt, pay attention to the thread in the bobbin as well as the speed of your hands coordinated with the machine's speed to help you solve those awful back problems.

HEAVIER THREAD CREATES BIGGER KNOTS.

A VISIT TO PROVENCE, 23" x 23½", BY THE AUTHOR. TRADITIONAL MARKED FEATHERS ARE STITCHED TWICE ON THE TIPS.

Skinny Threads

While pursuing the ideal "you can never be too thin or too rich," I realized that, while that was never going to happen to me in my lifetime, my machine quilting could definitely benefit from using skinny, expensive threads to produce a luxurious, lovely, delicious look.

All my early machine quilting was done with the thinnest thread available, monofilament nylon, also known as "invisible" thread. It creates the illusion of hand quilting, produces dimension, and makes mistakes almost undetectable. The quilter can use its invisible properties as "smoke and mirrors" to quilt over lines several times and fool the eye into believing it never happened. In addition, uneven stitches from a beginner's efforts will not be noticeable. This

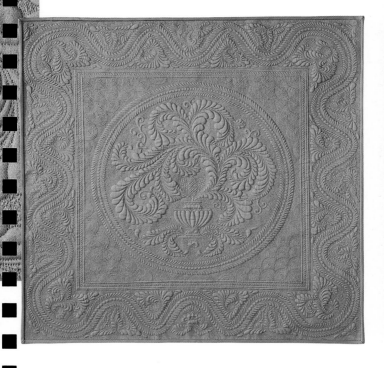

EXAMPLES OF SKINNY THREADS

thread was my "training wheels" for the opaque threads I use now.

As years went by and my quilting improved, I longed for the properties of invisible thread but with the luster and glow of opaque thread. Students in classes were bringing bins of tempting threads, glistening with saturated colors and silky textures. I wanted some, too. I tried various cottons and cringed. They jumped out at me from the quilt and detracted from the color and design of the fabrics. Cotton thread looks like kite string to my eyes. Even using #60 cotton was distressing to me. It seemed like trying to do ballet while wearing hiking boots!

I was looking for something thin and elegant but didn't know what it could be. Then I chanced upon a small basket of silk thread spools set out for the hand-appliqué crowd. Wheels started turning in my head, and I bought the #100, a very fine silk, in a neutral taupe color, then neglected it for months. One day, I noticed it languishing on the shelf and decided to give it a try. I have not looked back since that day and have quilted almost exclusively with this beautiful thread.

Because I am a devoutly frugal Midwesterner, at first it was difficult to pay the price for the expensive silk, especially compared to monofilament, but rationalization is one of my best abilities. Now I am grateful, because the expense of the silk is very much worth it in the long run. The old adage "you get what you pay for" is definitely true with silk thread in the results it provides. Lines of stitching can be quilted over to travel to another area in a quilt, and the two lines of stitching done with fine silk will read as one.

Simple designs that have points where many lines of stitching meet or cross can be problematic with heavier threads, but skinny threads solve this problem, too. No thread build-up occurs to form knots on the front of the quilt. Even a simple continuous-line

EXAMPLE OF INVISIBLE THREAD QUILTING

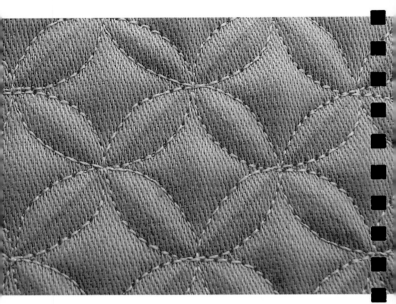

WITH FINE THREAD, THERE'S NO THREAD BUILD-UP WHERE THE STITCHING LINES CROSS.

design made for machine quilting may have a center point where as many as eight lines cross, building up a cone of thread in the center unless fine thread is used.

There are other skinny thread options besides silk. Most are formulated for bobbin use, but they can be used for quilting as well. Long-staple Egyptian cotton, fine-filament opaque polyester, even heavier silks are terrific for both bobbin and needle. Most thread companies are coming out with these finer threads, and machine quilters are paying the slightly higher price to get the results that really elevate their machine quilting from everyday to elegant and rich.

Color Choices

It's nice to have a big assortment of colors, but really, most of the neutrals will blend in beautifully with any fabric color. Neutral taupe can be used to quilt a variety of fabric colors, from chartreuse to gold to rose. The taupe becomes the color of the fabric, and it reflects the surrounding color. Plus it adds subtle highlights, giving extra dimension to the fabric color. It works much like highlighting hair and takes away the flatness that quilting with a matching thread can create. Silk has a wonderful capability to reflect light, so it adds more than color to a quilt; it adds subtle pizzazz.

With silk in the needle for quilting, you can use a variety of bobbin threads. A bobbin thread that is the same color and fiber as the top thread is ideal, so using silk in the bobbin works extremely well. The back of the quilt will look as beautiful and fine as the front, with no knots, lumps, or bumps. You can change the bobbin thread color as needed to match a variety of top thread colors, or you can use one neutral, such as taupe, tan, or ecru, in the bobbin for the whole quilt regardless of changes in the top thread color.

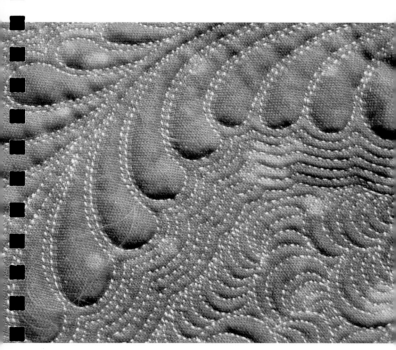

BACK OF QUILT, CAT HAIR A BONUS

A word of caution: using a high-contrast color of skinny thread does not look as nice as a heavier thread would. A #100 black silk thread on muslin looks terrible. A big difference in color, especially with dark thread on light fabric, shows any irregularities in the machine stitches, such as the slight wobble they sometimes have, especially when quilting away from yourself. Try to avoid this color combination and, instead, choose a fine thread that either matches the fabric or is one or two shades lighter or darker or a slightly different hue.

Because the effect achieved with fine silk thread is so subtle, several colors can be used successfully without their shouting that a color switch was made. For instance, I have quilted designs with copper and stippled around them with rose, which causes the background quilting to recede a bit from the designs.

ONE THREAD COLOR WAS USED FOR THE DESIGN
AND ANOTHER FOR THE BACKGROUND.

IT'S NOT NECESSARY TO MATCH THREAD COLORS.

Play with colors. Throw away preconceived ideas about the way the thread looks when it's on the spool. If you can't decide which thread color you prefer, use both. Work them into your designs in a planned way. Do the designs with one color and the background with the other. Try three or four different shades and see what a lovely effect they have on your machine quilting. We quilters have had to match thread color for so long that it's time to play with color and have fun.

Making a Mock-up

When picking out thread for a project, it is a wise quilter who takes the time to layer a small mock-up of the project's materials: top fabrics (pieced together), batt, and backing. Quilt different areas of the mock-up with various weights and colors of thread to see how they look off the spool. Thread looks different when it's used for quilting compared to using it on a single layer of fabric.

EXAMPLE OF A MOCK-UP

Also, if you plan to quilt a design, such as a feather, do one feather in each test thread so you can really compare them. The background stippling may look terrible in one color, but that same color may be perfect for feathers. You will find that all preconceived ideas about matching the thread to the quilt will fly out the window once you start working with fine threads.

After your mock-up has been made, it is really crucial to get it out of the machine and away from the light you use there. Hold the mock-up vertically under different lighting. Pin it to a wall or place it on the kitchen table so that, every time you walk past it, you get a fresh look. Usually the question about what thread to use answers itself when you have the chance to view it in many different lights and positions. Even your mood can effect the appearance.

If you begin work on the actual project and decide that a different color might be the wise choice, go for it. I have many times used a variety of colors on quilts when the original choice proved less than satisfactory. Because the change may be slight and visible only to you, leave in the original quilting and blend the new color choice with it. It is okay to change horses in mid-stream. Be open to all possibilities, and your quilting will reflect a new level of color sophistication.

Stitch Length

What about stitch length with skinny threads? A normal-sized, default stitch length is a bit too big for this delicate thread. Getting smaller stitches in free-motion quilting is as easy as stepping on the gas a bit; that is, using a higher motor speed but keeping your hand speed the same. Your stitches will get smaller, with no increased skill on your part. Don't tell people that small stitches are easy. Let them think you spent years working at getting them tiny. Now, even and consistent stitches are another story. That does take a bit of work.

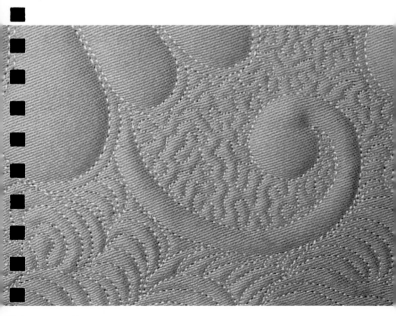

NOTICE THE SMALL STITCHES AROUND THE MOTIFS AND EVEN SMALLER STITCHES IN THE STIPPLING.

Longer stitches look spidery and wobbly. They show every little inconsistency that is inherent in a machine stitch. With thicker threads, such as #50 three-ply cotton, long a staple in machine quilting, a longer stitch length is not only possible but also preferable. The very bulk and thickness of the thread fills up the design or background area, and it looks smooth and full. Thin threads cannot do this, so they require you to use a much shorter stitch to get the same filled look. The advantage in the shorter stitch length is less wobble and it's smoother. Be aware though that it is all too easy to get stitches too small and then they pile up and look even worse than the longer stitches.

I use very fine threads for miniature quilts and for my detailed quilting in large quilts. If you decrease the stitch length, these finer threads can be used for any size of design, even very large overall meandering or pantograph-style patterns.

Don't think that, because you are a beginning machine quilter, you cannot use these threads. They can instantly take you to a more polished look. Silk thread is beautiful, and sewing machines love it. Used in both the needle and the bobbin, it provides a more refined quilting stitch than you ever thought possible.

Bobbin Thread Tension

You may need to change the bobbin tension to get the proper stitch quality if you use silk or very fine threads in the bobbin. Most bobbin screws will have to be tightened just a bit. Think of the screw as a clock face. Look at the position of the line on the bobbin screw and use a permanent marking pen to place a dot at this position before you do any adjusting. Then, if the line on the screw is

A VISIT TO PROVENCE (DETAIL). SILK THREAD QUILTING IS REFINED AND ELEGANT. THESE FEATHERS ARE FREEHAND, YET FORMAL.

ADJUSTING BOBBIN TENSION

pointing to 9 o'clock, tighten it to 10 o'clock. Do a test on your practice piece to see if the tension is better. Investing in a separate bobbin case just for skinny bobbin threads is an excellent idea, and your service person may be willing to adjust the bobbin for you if you are uncertain how to proceed.

Sometimes it takes a good half hour to get the top and bobbin tension just right, but it is definitely possible with a tuned-up machine in good working order and no other apparent problems. If the machine is working properly and you know how to adjust the tension, you can successfully use a different color in the needle and bobbin and not have the bobbin color pop up on the front.

> **TIP!** If you are making tension adjustments top and bottom, change only one at a time. Adjust the top tension first and see if that helps the stitch balance and quality, then adjust the bobbin tension, if necessary.

Troubleshooting

One thing skinny thread will tell you immediately is the existence of any problem with your machine. Using this delicate thread simply will not work if there are burrs, gouges in the throat plate or bobbin hook, timing disorders, problems with the bobbin or tension spring, or grooves worn into the metal parts by threads such as nylon monofilament. The skinny thread will get caught and fray or break. This thread is like a lie detector; it shows up everything. A poorly maintained and cleaned machine will have problems with this thread. Fortunately, most of these problems can be easily corrected by your service person if you explain what thread you are using and what the problem is.

If the thread frays constantly, the needle may be too small. Try going up one size (larger number). I like to use a #60 Microtex sharp with #100 silk thread, but sometimes the eye may be rough or the thread may have swelled a bit on a particularly damp day so that I have to use a #70 sharp to keep the thread from fraying.

Skipped stitches are usually caused by the same problem: the needle is too small. Go up one size and try again. Another cause of skipped stitches is a very flat batt, often used by machine quilters. For this batt, the pressure on the presser foot needs to be increased so the foot sits a bit tighter on the quilt but still allows the quilt to move freely. Owner's manuals often help with these adjustments.

Sometimes a waxy buildup will occur in your machine when you are using silk thread. Check the thread pathway often and use a cotton swab to gently remove any thread debris. In addition, I clean and oil the bobbin area every three hours to keep it running smoothly, and there is often this waxy substance there as well. Cleaning it takes minutes and prevents problems from occurring.

One of the benefits of using silk or other fine threads in the bobbin is that the bobbin thread lasts for hours and hours. In fact, you will have to remind yourself to stop in three hours to swab out the bobbin area and give it a drop of oil to keep things humming along. There will still be thread on the bobbin.

Don't Forget Playtime

Whenever you try new threads, it is going to mean a journey through uncharted territory with you and your machine. You may have to change settings, try new needles, and make smaller stitches. Set aside some time to play with the threads on various fabrics.

Switch colors. See how the very-fine threads allow you so much freedom in machine quilting. Have a fun afternoon, and don't try this on a deadline quilt when you are under pressure. The excitement of seeing the beauty that these threads create is well worth the effort and will renew your interest in machine quilting, taking it to a whole new level.

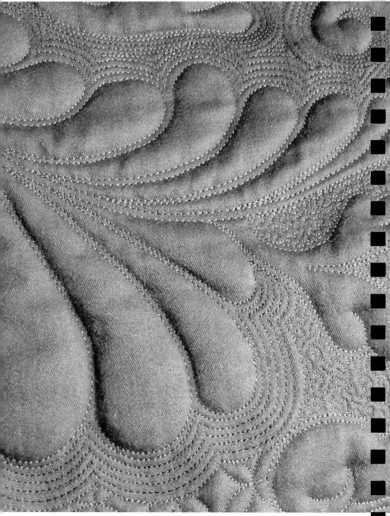

A VARIETY OF COLORS WERE USED IN THE ECHO QUILTING.

Tips for Quilting with Silk Thread

❖ You can pair silk thread in the needle with fine cotton thread, such as Egyptian long-staple cotton, in the bobbin.

❖ Space the quilting lines closer because the thread is so fine.

❖ You can start and stop by using seven or eight very closely spaced stitches and clipping the threads close to the quilt. It is almost impossible to remove this closely spaced stitching, so the quilting doesn't comes out.

❖ For walking-foot quilting, such as an all-over grid, use a shorter stitch length, for example a 1.50 setting, and keep the grid lines closer together, every 1" or so.

❖ Run some heavier cotton thread (#50) through the top of the machine every now and then to remove any residue.

SUGGESTED FINE THREADS

Here is a list of some great fine threads for you to try for your needle and your bobbin. Remember, many of these threads "read" finer than the number on the spool.

YLI Soft Touch #60 Egyptian cotton

Aurifil® #50 Egyptian cotton

Mettler® #60 2-ply cotton

DMC® #50 cotton

YLI #100 silk

Superior Bottom Line™

Superior MasterPiece™ cotton

Trapunto

Back in the early '90s, I picked up a quilt magazine and found a short, interesting article written by Hari Walner, one of our early pioneers in machine quilting and continuous-line designs. I read it with my usual skepticism. It explained a new technique for stuffing machine-quilted designs by using a water-soluble thread to baste the batting to the back of the designs. The quilt was then layered with a cotton batt and backing.

Now, after ten years of working with this technique, it is my friend. I have learned its little ways. I know when and how to use it and all the tricks and tips to make the most of this technique. Note that, while this technique can be used with quilts done on home machines, machines in frames, or longarm machines, the following information will pertain only to home machine quilting. If used with other setups, the limitations are much fewer because the quilt does not have to be rolled to fit into the opening of a home sewing machine.

> **TIP!** This technique may also be used to stuff appliqués.

Basic Method

❖ First, mark all the quilt designs then place a piece of polyester batt under each design to be stuffed.

❖ Pin the batt in place and use free-motion quilting to sew around the outside of the design with water-soluble thread. The thread will wash out later.

❖Turn the top over and trim away any batting that is not under a design, leaving each design with an underlay of batting.

❖In the usual way, layer the quilt with cotton batting and backing then pin baste. Use your choice of thread to quilt the layers.

❖When finished, submerge the quilt in cool water. The water-soluble thread will dissolve, the cotton batt will shrink somewhat, and the design will be stuffed with the poly batt, enhanced by the shrinkage of the cotton batt. Voilá! You will have stuffed designs with the speed and power of a sewing machine.

Choosing a Design

There are traditional designs, like feathered wreaths, that make wonderful choices for this trapunto technique, as well as more contemporary continuous-line designs. However, there are some considerations to keep in mind when choosing a design for trapunto:

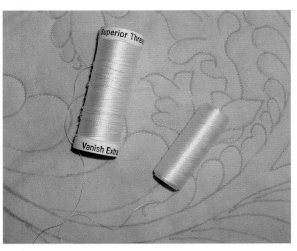

QUILT AROUND THE DESIGN WITH WATER-SOLU-BLE THREAD.

Is it easy to quilt? Some designs that would look fantastic stuffed are very difficult to machine quilt, such as traditional feathers. Determine what skill level you want for machine quilting and keep this in mind when picking a design. A feathered plume might look beautiful and be easy to trim, but it is more difficult to machine quilt. There are some designs that combine the best of both: easy to trim, easy to quilt, and a lot of effect for the work.

Is it too time consuming to trim? Some wonderful continuous-line designs in your area of expertise that are easy to quilt will take forever to trim, with winding lines and long skinny areas in between. For your first try, look for a simple design to quilt that doesn't have a lot of little hard-to-reach areas that need trimming. The design must also have an outer edge and not consist of only intertwining lines.

The bigger the design shapes, the more you will see the trapunto. A large feather shape will look more stuffed than a very small one. Sometimes the designs have such small stuffed areas that the trapunto doesn't show.

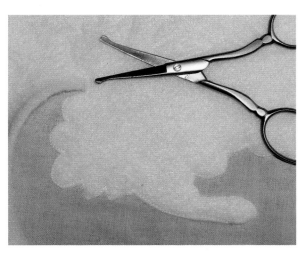

TRIM BATTING FROM AROUND THE DESIGN.

Placement of Trapunto

How much trapunto you add to a quilt top and where you add it are important in how the quilt will look and behave when finished.

Use trapunto throughout the quilt, if possible, so one area doesn't pull in more and distort the quilt. A simple quilt with many trapuntoed designs in the border surrounded by very close stippling will result in the borders shrinking in too much. Then the center will balloon out and the quilt will not hang well. The reverse is true as well. Too much trapunto in the center and none in the borders will cause wavy borders.

Be careful not to add so much trapunto to a large quilt that it will be too thick and puffy to roll up and fit in your sewing machine.

Choosing Batting

There are two battings to consider when doing trapunto: the one used to stuff the designs and a batt used for the entire quilt. The batting used for the trapunto can be any type of polyester, or really even several layers of cotton blend or wool batting, but polyester seems to give the most effect. It doesn't shrink, and it works the best with the underlying cotton batt. You can always experiment with various combinations of batt to get the look you want and the materials you like.

A very thick, puffy "fat" batt can be used effectively, but watch out if you are using it throughout a large-sized quilt because it might become too bulky to fit through the arm of a home sewing machine. A fat batt is also difficult to quilt, much like machine quilting a marshmallow. The flatter, denser poly batts seem to work the best. They don't add as much bulk to the project, and a free-motion foot is able to clear them without "snowplowing" or getting hung up on the added bulk. I look for a poly batt that is thin, dense, and easy to trim, such as Fairfield's Traditional®, or Quilter's Dream® Select Poly. Make a sample first before committing to an entire quilt. If the result isn't stuffed enough, try doubling the poly layers to add more loft in the designs.

Be sure the batting is easy to trim with scissors. Some batts, like fleece, are difficult to cut and shouldn't be used. Some are thick like cotton candy and take many cuts to get through all the frizzy layers. This trapunto method requires much trimming away of the polyester batt from around the designs so the batt must be easy to cut. You need to cut close to the line of stitching so there isn't any messy overhang or "whiskers."

Watch out for bearding. One of my favorite polyester batts had all the perfect characteristics: thin, dense, easily available, easy to trim, firmly filled the design, and not too puffy to quilt through. It was my batt of choice until I used it under a dark quilt top and discovered that it migrated through the quilt-top fabrics and bearded, leaving long wisps of fiber all over the quilt, very unsightly and difficult to remove. Many times you can determine if there is a right or wrong side to the poly batt. Place the smoothest side facing up.

Make sure the batting is slippery and that it will move well on the bed of your sewing machine. You will be doing the preliminary stitching around the designs with no backing on the quilt and the feed dogs lowered. Some batts grip the surface and will not slide easily. Do a test with various batts to find one that does move easily.

Stitching the Design

Once you have the designs on the quilt top completely marked, layer the top over the poly batt and pin around the designs. Sometimes there will be so many designs you want stuffed that it is easiest to simply use a poly batt under the entire quilt top. For spot trapunto, pin small pieces of batt under each design. You are now ready to free-motion quilt around the perimeter of each design with water-soluble thread. Use water-soluble thread in the bobbin as well. Use a slower speed when winding the bobbin so the thread doesn't break. Interior lines in designs will be done with quilting thread later.

Reduce the top tension just a bit so the thread doesn't break. This is very fine thread and it can be fragile, so a lower tension helps keep it from breaking when going through the machine. Use a new needle. I use a #60 or #70 Microtex sharp, which leaves only a fine hole in the quilt.

Check for any rough spots or burrs in the opening of the throat plate where the bobbin thread comes through. If it is gouged or nicked and rough, the bobbin thread will get caught and free-motion quilting will be difficult, even impossible, with water-soluble thread.

Run the machine a little slower than you normally do for machine quilting. It's okay if the stitches are too large or uneven, because they will wash out.

Check the tension as you go along. If the top tension is too tight, the design will pull in and distort the quilt top. If you find this happening, snip the stitches every inch or so when you are trimming the poly on the back, or give the design a gentle corner-to-corner tug and hear the threads snap and break. The design should lie smooth and flat when trimmed. If it pulls in and distorts now, when you quilt it, there will be pleats stitched in around the design.

Try to place the basting stitches on the marked line or just inside it. You don't have to lock in or secure these stitches. When you quilt the design, stitch exactly on the line or on the outside so you will enclose all of the poly batt. It's easier to see what you are doing and get good stitches if you aren't stitching directly over the water-soluble stitches, especially in designs like feathers.

TIP! Don't lick the water-soluble thread when you thread the needle!

Trimming

The next step is trimming the excess poly batt from around the quilting designs on the back of the quilt. This task gives machine quilters some lap work finally. It can be done while watching TV, being with the family, or in your favorite recliner with a good reading light, but don't daydream here or you will find that a cut can so easily be made in the quilt top, necessitating some very creative "fixes."

Use very sharp scissors and have several pairs that you can alternate using so your hands don't get too sore, or even blister. The new squeeze-type scissors with no loops for finger and thumb are wonderful for trimming trapunto. Some quilters choose appliqué scissors with a large flap to keep from cutting through the top of the quilt, or very sharp scissors but with blunt or rounded ends.

When trimming and using sharp-tipped scissors to get into all the little nooks and crannies, I usually keep one hand under the quilt top and by touch can tell if the scissors tip is coming through.

Trim as close to the stitching as possible. There should be a nice sharp dividing line between stuffed and unstuffed areas so you can see the difference in thickness.

Take breaks when trimming. It can be extremely fatiguing to muscles you normally don't use in sewing or quilting.

Batting scraps can be saved and used for stuffing pillows or toys, or added to the sagging back or seats of upholstered chairs, like your husband's favorite recliner.

Layering the Quilt

The polyester batt under the trapuntoed designs on the quilt top actually helps keep the top from slipping when pinning and quilting it. The trapunto batt acts like glue and holds the layers together. However, the quilt must still be pin-basted carefully, even in the interior of the designs, so that "snow-plowing," that is, pushing the excess quilt top fabric along, will not occur to form pleats. Pin normally, about 4" to 5" apart, being careful to pin in the interior of the designs and around the outside as well to keep them from shifting while being quilted.

> **TIP!** Store water-soluble thread and the wound bobbin together in a zippered bag to keep moisture from harming the thread. Also, after you use water-soluble thread, take it out of your machine. You just might forget and quilt with it.

Quilting the Layers

The added bulk of extra polyester under the designs or other parts of your quilt will make quilting a bit more difficult. However, you should be able to roll the quilt just as you would if it didn't have trapunto.

Do the stabilizing quilting first. Then quilt the flat areas that have no trapunto. Quilt the trapunto designs on the marked lines or on the outside edge of the marked lines, ignoring the basting stitches with water-soluble thread. If you focus on these stitches instead of the quilting lines, you will get confused and your quilting will reflect it.

If your machine has an adjustment that will allow you to raise the presser foot or reduce its pressure, this will help the foot glide smoothly over the extra stuffing under the designs. Even with the added trapunto, the quilt should move freely under the foot. Some machines have special free-motion or quilting feet that sit a little bit higher off the quilt and allow you to make quilts with thicker batts or with trapunto.

For the trapunto to be noticeable and effective, it must be surrounded by closely spaced background quilting. This background quilting makes the trapunto stand out. It can be stippling, straight lines ¼" apart, echo quilting, cross-hatch grid quilting, or any other close quilting design you want to do, such as clamshells.

If you stipple, be sure to quilt right up to the design and bump into it with the stippling shapes. This will flatten the background and any whiskers of poly bat outside the stitched design. It will also make the trapunto design stand out. The stippling shapes should be smaller than the smallest design shape in the quilting design itself. Small feathers mean even smaller stippling. Large feathers may be surrounded with larger stippling shapes. Proportion is important, or the designs will be lost and the trapunto effect minimized.

> **TIP!** A few simple lines of echo quilting around a design will allow you to use larger-scale stippling.

Finishing Touches

When the quilting is finished and the quilt has been bound, it has to be completely submerged in cool water for several minutes and agitated gently for the thread to dissolve and the markings to disappear. To completely remove any traces of starch, marking chemicals, and thread residue, wash the quilt in warm water in the delicate cycle of your washer with a small amount of quilt soap.

To enhance the trapunto designs further, the quilt can be dried for a few minutes or

THE BACKGROUND QUILTING NEEDS TO TOUCH THE TRAPUNTO.

until almost dry on low heat in the dryer. The heat causes the cotton batt to shrink even more and push the poly batt up and into the trapunto design. Lay the quilt flat to finish drying. When dry, the quilt will have marvelous dimension from the trapunto you have added.

Additional Considerations

It's a good idea to make some small samples, such as pillows or potholders, to test your materials and techniques. It's the combination of the batts and the shrinkage of the cotton underlying the trapunto when washed that produces the results. Try various combinations until you find one that looks right to you, and one that fits under the foot on your sewing machine and moves easily for quilting.

This technique works for marked designs. If you hate to mark, you won't like doing trapunto. You must do background quilting or you will not be able to notice that the designs are stuffed.

If you want, you can do the trapunto on setting squares in a quilt before it is pieced together. Be careful when sewing the top together with the trapuntoed squares to avoid pressing any wash-out blue markings. Keep the designs about ½" or more from the edges of the blocks. If the trapunto is only on the borders, cut strips of poly batting and apply them only under the borders, doing one side of the quilt at a time.

Hari Walner's method of trapunto has revolutionized the look of machine-quilted tops. It's quite a bit of extra work in a large quilt and does add weight and thickness, making the quilt more difficult to handle. Try it out on something small first, like the Trapunto Tee project on page 134, to learn all about it and see how you like it.

Trapunto Tee

U sing a simple tee shirt and modified machine trapunto techniques, in a very short time, you will be able to create a garment to sneak under a business suit, wear with casual clothing, or use as a group project. Choose a motif, a logo, your own design, or any small stencil design for the front of the tee. If you are feeling adventurous, add another to the back, the shoulder area, the hemline, or wherever you want a little extra something. This shirt also makes an excellent gift. It is inexpensive, and it takes only a short time to create. Get out your water-soluble thread and your designs, and enjoy.

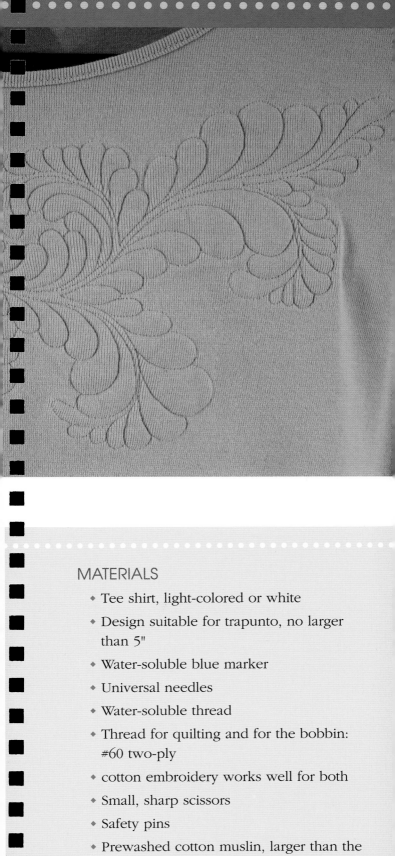

MATERIALS

- ◆ Tee shirt, light-colored or white
- ◆ Design suitable for trapunto, no larger than 5"
- ◆ Water-soluble blue marker
- ◆ Universal needles
- ◆ Water-soluble thread
- ◆ Thread for quilting and for the bobbin: #60 two-ply
- ◆ cotton embroidery works well for both
- ◆ Small, sharp scissors
- ◆ Safety pins
- ◆ Prewashed cotton muslin, larger than the design

There are a few differences from the traditional trapunto technique for machine quilting the tee. For one thing, there is no additional cotton batt under the design, just a simple piece of prewashed muslin. Also, the good news is there is no background quilting at all—no stippling, no grids, no echo quilting. The motif will be plump and will stand out on its own on the tee.

This project will teach you some good new machine quilting skills. One is to slow down a bit to manipulate the tee over the small free-arm section of your machine. Also, you will have to move the tee with your fingertips because of the small workspace, and it will teach you the way to quilt with a little less pushing and pulling and more dexterity.

Instructions

1. Prewash an inexpensive or old tee shirt and pick a design to trace on the center front. A continuous-line design works well. Try not to choose designs that contain straight lines for this project.

2. Trace the design on the front of the tee with a blue washout marker. I found I could trace the design on a light-colored tee without a light box. However, you might have to use or make a stencil. Secure the stencil to the tee with masking tape.

3. Cut a piece of thin, flat polyester batt and insert it under the design area. Safety pin it in place around the design, being careful to place your hand behind the batt so you don't pin through to the back of the tee (fig. 1).

4. Clean out the area under the free arm of your machine to make sure there isn't any

oil or anything that will catch or stain your tee. Don't ask how I know this.

5. Using the machine trapunto technique and water-soluble thread in the top and bobbin, free-motion baste around the outside of the design. Do not go into any interior detail lines of the design, and be sure the back of the tee shirt is under the free arm.

6. Turn the tee inside out, and carefully trim the excess batt from around the design with sharp scissors. Use your other hand to feel under the design and keep the scissors points from coming through and cutting the tee fabric.

PINNED DESIGN, BASTED AND READY TO QUILT

7. Cut a piece of prewashed muslin bigger than your design. Insert it behind the design and pin it in place with safety pins. (Do not add cotton batt under the design as you would for a quilt.)

8. Put quilting thread in your machine. I quilted mine with #100 silk thread in the top and #60 cotton in the bobbin, but you could certainly use metallic, variegated, rayon, heavier silk, or embellishing thread. Pick a universal needle to go along with whatever size thread you choose.

9. Position the tee around the free arm and quilt the design. It is difficult to get straight lines on tee fabric, so don't worry if your quilting looks wavy. It will look fine when it's done.

10. Trim the muslin close to the design, about ⅛" to ¼" away from the quilting line. The edge will ravel with washing and wear, but it won't be a problem.

11. Soak the tee in cool water to remove the water-soluble threads and blue marking and wash the tee shirt in warm water with a little soap. Dry on low in the dryer until almost dry. Spread the tee flat and smooth the design to finish drying.

Wear it and enjoy the compliments!

Trapunto Tee
FULL-SIZED PATTERN

141

Acknowledgments

A huge thank you to all who have helped make this book possible, from the quilters of the past who inspire me, to the modern quilters who work wonders on their sewing machines. Special thanks to:

Marjie Russell, my *American Quilter* editor, who had faith in me and my writing and told me that quilters wanted to know more;

Barbara Smith, my book editor, who takes all my wanderings and makes them orderly, understandable, and interesting, and who is endlessly patient;

Rosemary Malzahn, my "manager," who gives me ideas to run with;

Everyone at Bigsby's Sewing Center, who is always there for me;

Bernina of America, and especially Gayle Hillert, for their unstinting support;

Carol Selepec, who told me to "get going and make another miniature";

Bill Schroeder, for his warmth and caring, and support of quilting;

My mother, Erma Hinterberg, who taught me to sew;

My dear friends who listen, always; and

Everyone at AQS for their support and encouragement, and excellence in their work.

About the Author

A master quilter, Diane began machine quilting in 1988, after growing up with lovingly hand-quilted scrap quilts from her grandmother. Diane is known for her original feather designs and intensive quilting based on historic quilts. Perfecting the technique of traditional machine quilting has taken more than 20 years of work and experimenting, and presently, her work is shown internationally, has won numerous prestigious awards, and is in private collections and museums.

A Wisconsin native, Diane teaches and judges locally and nationally, has appeared on many television programs, and is the author of *Guide to Machine Quilting* (AQS 2002), as well as numerous articles for magazines, including *American Quilter, Quilter's Newsletter Magazine,* and *Threads.*

For more information, visit her Web site, www.dianegaudynski.net.

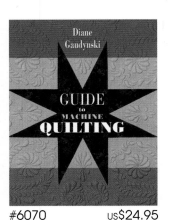

 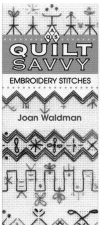 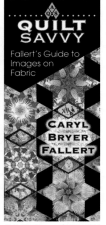